THE VIOLIN

Learn to Play

THE VIOLIN

An Illustrated
Step-by-Step
Instructional Guide

Frank Cappelli

ELDORADO INK

Eldorado Ink
PO Box 100097
Pittsburgh, PA 15233
www.eldoradoink.com

Copyright © 2010 by Eldorado Ink. All rights reserved.
Printed and bound in Malaysia.

CPSIA compliance information: Batch#101909-14. For further information,
contact Eldorado Ink at info@eldoradoink.com.

 3 5 7 9 8 6 4 2

Library of Congress Cataloging-in-Publication Data

    Cappelli, Frank.
     The violin / Frank Cappelli.
       p. cm. — (Learn to play)
     Includes bibliographical references and index.
     ISBN-13: 978-1-932904-17-8
     ISBN-10: 1-932904-17-4
     1. Violin—Methods. I. Title.
     MT262.C25 2007
     787.2'193—dc22

                      2006037094

For information about custom editions, special sales, or premiums,
please contact our special sales department at info@eldoradoink.com.

Acknowledgements

The author would like to thank all of those who provided instruments to
be used in the photographs of this book, particularly Volkwein's Music
of Pittsburgh (800-553-8742; www.volkweins.com).

TABLE OF CONTENTS

Part Three: Let's Play!

Part Four: Songs

Clarinet
Flute
Guitar
Piano
Trumpet
Violin

INTRODUCTION

Many people love the beautiful, clear sound of a violin being played by a skilled musician. Stringed instruments have a long history, but no one is sure when the first violin was made or how it came to be developed. Historians have pointed to ancient instruments that had three, four, or five strings as the ancestors of the violin. Instruments like the ancient lyre, an Indian instrument called the robob, and an Arab instrument called the rebec all look similar in one way or another to the violin. And they could all be considered part of the evolution of the violin.

It is unknown where the first violin in its modern form was made. There are paintings from the early 1500s that show the instrument, so we must assume that they were made in the late 1400s to the early 1500s. What we do know is that in a small town in Italy called Cremona in the early 1500s violins like the ones we know today were being made. The Cremonese craftsmen may have been the original inventors. But even if they were not, their instruments were a milestone in violin development.

One of the great violinmakers of Cremona was a man named Andrea Amati. It is believed he lived between 1535 and 1611 and was the founder of the world's most famous school of violin-making. Great violinmakers like Guarneri and Stradivari learned their trade from the Amati family and their school.

By the late 1600s violins and violin-making had become popular all over Europe. Yet despite the hundreds of violinmakers that have worked over the years, the instruments made by Stradivari and Guarneri remain the most desired concert instruments by great musicians. Unfortunately they have become so rare that they are almost too valuable to play.

Learning how to play the violin will take a lot of practice and determination, but the rewards will be worth the time and effort. This book presents a fresh approach to learning the violin, which will enable you to learn how to play and enjoy this wonderful instrument. Whether you are a true beginner, have a bit of musical training, or are a skilled musician on another instrument, the carefully developed approach of this book can help anyone succeed.

PART ONE: Getting Started

This book is intended for the beginning violin player. Anyone can play the violin; as with most other things in life, the level of success you will achieve depends on how much time you want to put into learning how to play.

To become a good violinist, you need to work hard and practice. Give yourself time and always look for new ways to make yourself better. One way to do this is to listen to your favorite songs and see whether you can pick out notes or melodies that you can play on your own. Even if you can't play the entire song at first, this kind of practicing will improve your skill. Also, play with other musicians whenever you get the chance. You will learn from them as they will learn from you.

You will experience exhilaration and frustration as you learn to understand and master the violin. Hopefully the way this book is structured will make your experience as stress-free as possible. The instructions, diagrams, and illustrations will help you through everything from the purchase of a violin to playing your first songs.

1. Choosing a Violin

The violin is a stringed instrument played with a bow. It has four strings, an unfretted fingerboard, and a shallow body. The violin's wide musical range makes it suitable for many playing styles.

The violin can play a range of notes that covers at least three octaves. (An octave consists of eight sequential notes in a scale, where the first note is one-half the frequency of the last note.) Violins can vary in size for bigger or smaller players, but they are usually about 24 inches (61 centimeters) long.

When you go to select a violin for yourself, choose one that feels good. The best thing to do is to go to a music store or a violin store and hold the

violins. Play the instrument and ask the salespeople questions. If you can go to more than one store, do that as well. They may have different sizes or brands.

You may wish to ask questions like:

1. What is the proper instrument size to buy?
2. What is the difference between types of violins?
3. What is the cost? Can I rent one instead of buying it?

To start out, you should get an instrument that feels comfortable when you hold it. One way to tell if the violin fits you is to place it under your chin and extend your left arm out. If you can curl your fingers over the top of the scroll of the violin and easily touch the tuning pegs, then that is a good size for you. If you can only just reach the top of the violin, then it may be a bit too large.

Compare the way different violins feel when you press the strings; some will be easier than others. Today there are many companies that make wonderful violins, so there will be a good variety to choose from. It is important that you find one that you will want to play, one that will encourage you to play.

The Electric Violin

For years, the only way to hear a violin in a band was to have the violin player lean into a microphone or attach a pickup to the violin to amplify the sound. Today, an instrument called an electric violin is becoming more popular as technology improves the sound.

The electric violin has all the parts of a regular violin except for the body. Electric violins are similar to electric guitars in that they have all the electronics necessary to produce sound built into a solid body. Compared to a classical violin, the body of an electric violin can be quite radical in appearance.

From the 1960s through the 1980s, the only way to hear an electric violin—if you could find one—was to plug it into an amplifier. Now, an electric violin can be plugged into a computer to produce sound.

The best way for you to know whether you'd like an electric violin is go to a music store and try a number of different types of instruments and amps. Today companies make amplifiers that are small with a low wattage, which are nice for practicing or playing with a friend. If you intend to play in a band or need the amplifier to make the violin carry over other musicians, you may need an amplifier that has high wattage.

An electric violin is no more difficult to learn than a standard violin. Depending on the quality of standard violin you are considering, it might even be a cheaper option. What is most important is choosing an instrument that you will be inspired to pick up every day and practice.

2. Getting to Know the Violin

Let's take a look at the parts of a violin. The top of the violin is called the head, and it is topped by the scroll. At the top you will also find the tuning pegs, which are turned to change the sound of the strings.

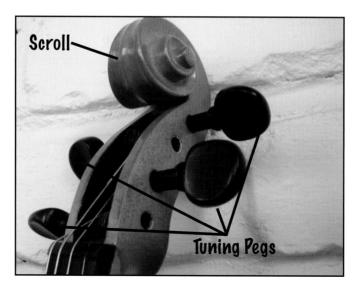

The neck goes from the head to the body. The neck is largely taken up by the fingerboard, which is where you place your fingers to produce different notes. Unlike the neck of a guitar, there are no frets on a violin.

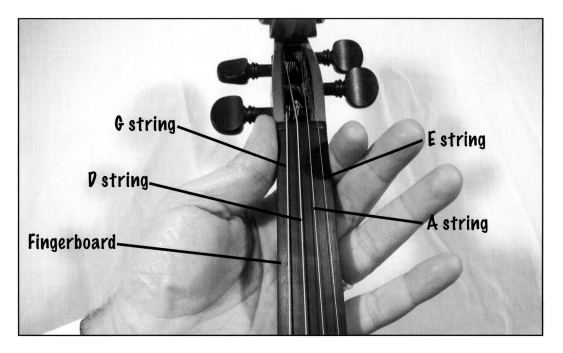

The violin body is hollow, which helps to amplify the sound of the strings when they are played. The type of wood that the body is made of, as well as the dimensions and shape of the body, determine how the instrument will sound. The F holes allow the sound to escape the violin body. The bridge elevates the strings and holds them in place.

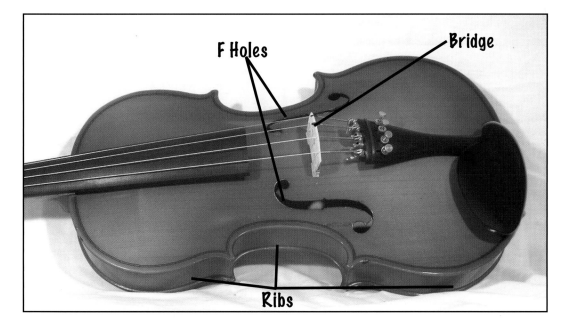

The sides of the body are called the ribs. It is important to make sure that the ribs don't crack or come loose.

Below the bridge is the tail piece, which holds the strings and fine tuners. The fine tuners enable the violinist to tune the strings properly.

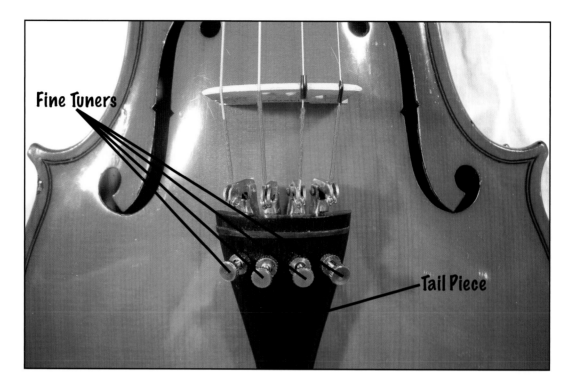

The chin rest is attached to the lower part of the body. It helps the violinist hold the instrument properly. The button, located at the bottom of the tailpiece, helps to hold everything in place.

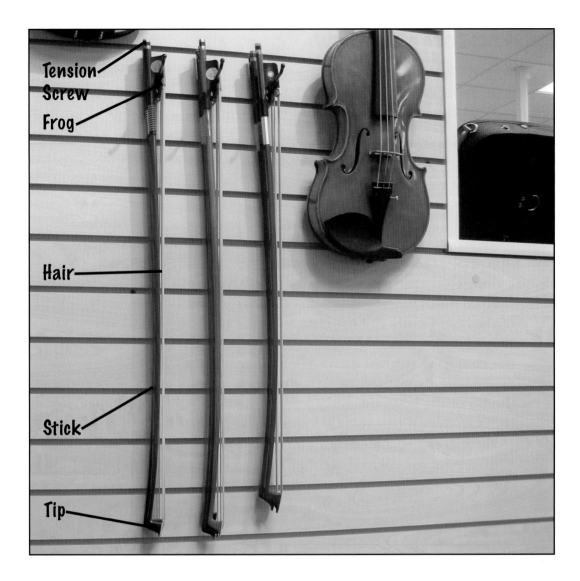

To play the violin, you use a bow. The parts of the bow are the tip, the stick, the hair, the frog, and the tension screw. The hair is the part of the bow that actually touches the strings to produce the notes. It must be kept at a certain tension in order to sound right. This is done by turning the tension screw, which draws the hair through the frog.

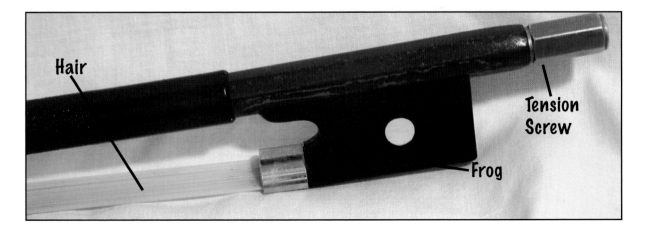

3. Taking Care of the Bow

Like a violin, the bow is a delicate instrument. It must be handled carefully so that it produces the proper sound and does not become damaged. Here are some guidelines to follow to care for the bow.

1. Before playing, tighten the bow by gently turning the tension screw. Don't make the bow hairs too tight—the space between the bow stick and hair at the closest point should be about the width of a pencil.

2. After you have tightened the tension screw, put a small amount of rosin on your bow. The rosin gives the bow friction, and it's the friction that produces the sound when you draw the bow over the strings.

    To do this, place the bow hairs flat on the cake of rosin at the frog of the bow. Gently rub the bottom of the bow back and forth a few times, like you are rubbing to get a stain out of a carpet. Then draw the bow hairs straight across the rosin cake until you reach the tip of the bow. Repeat the same back-and-forth rubbing movement at the tip of the bow, and then pull the bow across the rosin back to the frog. Repeat this several times.

    There aren't specific requirements for how often or how long to rosin a bow, but there is a simple test to determine if the bow has enough rosin. Using the back of your thumbnail, scrape under the hair of the bow near the frog). If you see a small puff of rosin, the bow is ready.

3. After each playing session, use a soft, dry cloth to remove rosin dust from the strings and body of the instrument.

4. When you are done playing, always loosen the hair on your bow by gently turning the tension screw.

5. Always store your violin and bow in its case.

A cake of rosin, which is rubbed on the hairs of the violin bow.

4. Holding the Violin

The violin is held horizontally (parallel with the floor) and is angled slightly to the left, as shown above. Place the violin so your left shoulder is well under the violin and rest the left side of your jaw on the chin rest. Your nose, the strings, your left elbow, and your left foot should all line up.

The left elbow should be under the center of the violin. Keep the wrist gently rounded. Avoid resting your left wrist against the violin's neck. The thumb should be opposite the first or second finger. Maintain a curved, open space between the thumb and index finger (a backwards "C").

Violinists use shoulder rests to help hold the violin in the proper position. There are a variety of commercially made shoulder rests available, although some violinists create their own using round make-up sponges and attach them to the violin with rubber bands. Find whatever works best for you.

When standing, be sure to stand straight with your feet shoulder width apart and your knees relaxed. Some violinists recommend sliding the left foot slightly forward. When seated, use a chair with a firm base and sit up straight (soft sofas aren't recommended). Some violinists sit towards the front of the chair and prefer placing the left foot slightly forward.

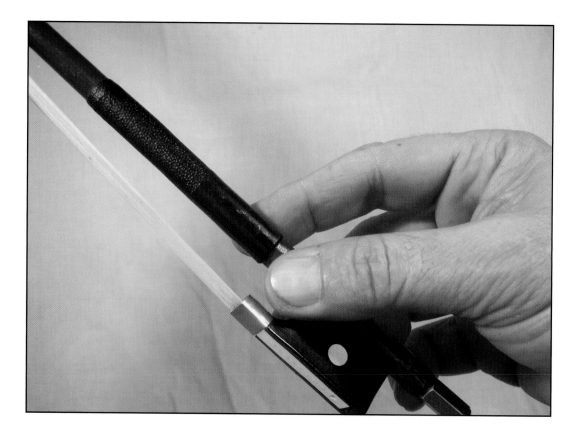

5. Holding the Bow

To hold the bow, relax your right hand and slightly turn your wrist to the left, letting the fingers droop. The tip of the thumb should curl slightly over the end of the frog. The fingers should curve gently around the top of the bow stick. Make sure the middle finger is opposite the thumb.

To produce a good tone, the right amount of pressure must be applied to the bow as it is drawn across the string. The speed of the bow is also important in creating the proper sound. You will get a feel for the proper pressure and speed through practice; for now, apply a slight downward pressure on the bow and draw it steadily across the strings.

HELPFUL TIP:
The sound of a violin is affected by the placement of the bow in relation to the bridge. There is a "sweet spot" that you will come to know with practice.

6. Changing the Strings

Most violinists keep an extra set of strings in their violin case, so they are prepared when a string breaks. Changing the strings is usually done one string at a time. Don't remove all of the strings on a violin at the same time or the soundpost and bridge could fall out of place.

If your instrument has a fine tuner, put the ball or loop end of the string over the tuner cartridge in the tailpiece (figure 1) and pull the string toward the bridge (figure 2). If the violin does not have a fine tuner, insert the ball or knotted end of the string through the tailpiece string hole, tug firmly to make sure the knot or ball is in the slot, and pull the string toward the bridge. Hold on to the ball or knot with your finger when you start turning the tuning peg.

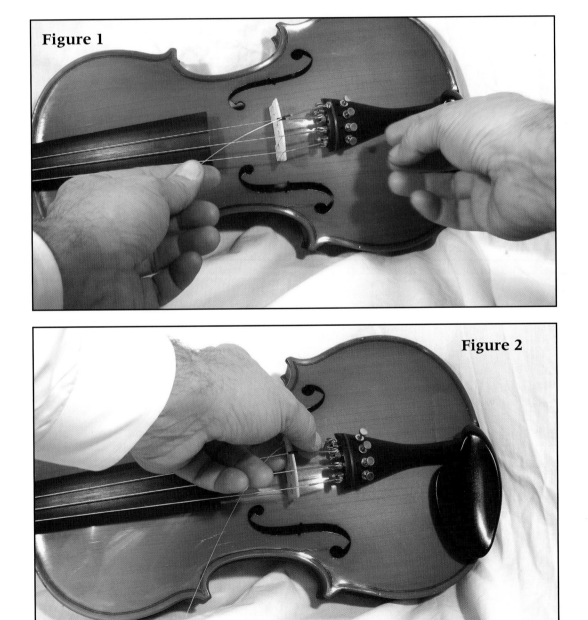

Figure 1

Figure 2

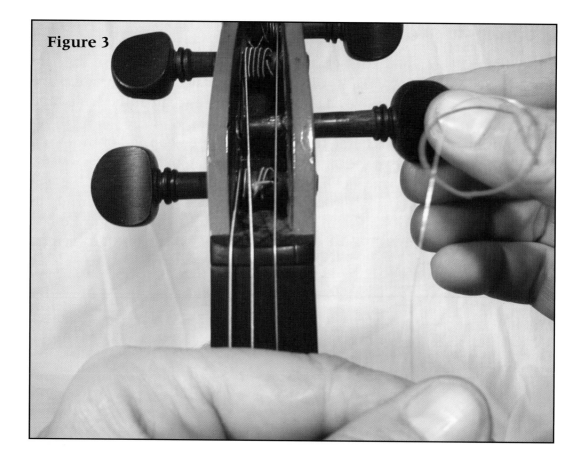

Figure 3

Pull out the tuning peg a bit (figure 3) as you thread the string through its eye (figure 4), and then slowly and gently push the peg into the peg hole.

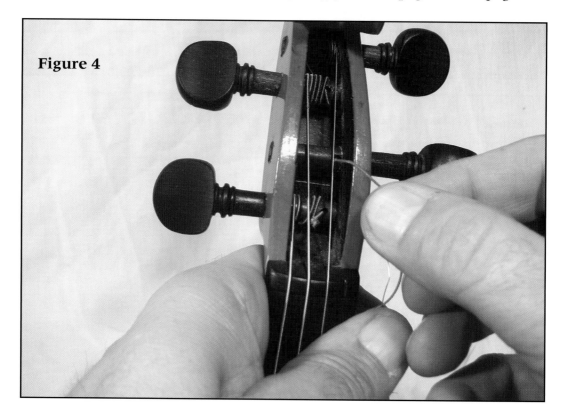

Figure 4

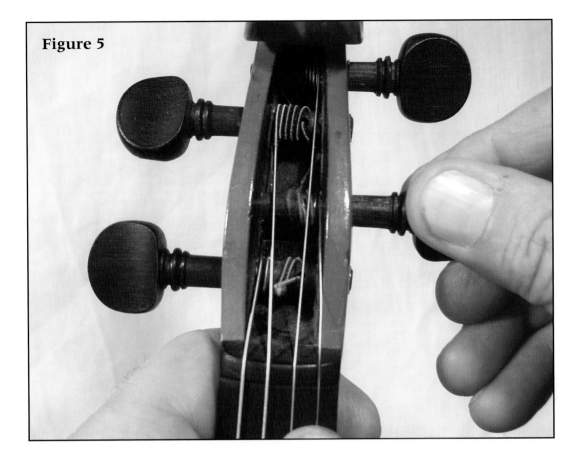

Figure 5

Put the end of the string through the peg hole (let a little of the string show), winding it very evenly (figure 5). Do not let the string overlap itself as you wind.

If your pegs are slipping or are too tight to securely adjust the strings, you may want to purchase peg compound (also called "peg dope"), an inexpensive commercial product.

If you don't have peg compound and need a temporary quick fix for slipping or tight pegs, here are some tips you can try. If a peg is sticking, pull it partially out and rub pencil graphite on it so that it turns more easily. If the peg is loose, try rubbing candle wax on it to help it stick.

7. Other Violin Care Tips

Extreme temperatures, particularly heat, can damage a violin, so be careful where you store it. Dryness can cause wooden violins to crack, so if you live in an area with a dry climate you may need to use a special humidifier to preserve your instrument.

If you want to polish your violin, only use a commercial violin polish. Trying to clean the violin with furniture polish and/or water could damage the varnish on the violin and negatively affect the instrument's acoustics.

Water could also cause the violin's seams to open. A violin does not need to be polished frequently.

Occasionally, you may find that you have to adjust the violin's bridge, which is held in place by the pressure of the strings, rather than glue. The bridge should be even with the fingerboard and stand straight up, perpendicular to the violin. The feet of the bridge should be aligned with the F-holes. The lower side of the bridge should be placed under the E string (the string with the highest pitch).

To adjust a tilting bridge, first slightly loosen the violin strings, then grasp the top of the bridge at its upper corners with the thumb and index fingers of each hand, and gently pull or push the top of the bridge until a 90° angle is achieved. If your bridge has become warped (or if you feel uncomfortable adjusting it yourself), take your violin to a local violin shop or instrument dealer for professional assistance.

HELPFUL TIP:
The violin is a difficult instrument to play, so be patient and don't be too hard on yourself. Regularly reminding yourself that learning how to play the violin will take a lot of time may help you to keep from getting frustrated.

PART TWO:

Reading Music

With what you will learn in this section, you will be able to communicate with musicians all around the world. I'll make it as painless as possible, but you've got to put in some time.

1. The Staff

The following will introduce you to some very basic concepts that will help you understand the notes on the violin. First, music is a language, and it is written on a staff. A staff has five lines and four spaces.

The lines and spaces are named starting at the bottom and going up, as illustrated by the staff below.

To give order to the music, the staff is divided into measures. A vertical line called a bar is used to mark out the measures. You know you're at the end of a section of music when you see a double bar line on the staff. Here is the staff with a G clef (also called a treble clef) with a 4/4 time signature and double bar line.

The double bar line tells a musician that he or she is at the end of a section or strain of music. Sometimes, however, there will be two dots before the double bar line. That means to repeat the section of music.

One other thing you may see when you are reading music is a small number at the beginning of some measures (circled in red below). This is just a helpful guide for the musician; it lets you know what measure you are playing. This can be particularly useful when you are playing music with a group and the leader or instructor wants you to start at a particular measure, rather than at the beginning of the song. Although in this book the number appears above the staff at the first measure of each line of music, in other music you may find that the number appears at the bottom of the staff, or that each measure is numbered.

Repeat Sign

2. The Notes

Next we shall take a look at what gets written on the staff. The notes tell us what tones to play and take on the names of the lines or spaces they occupy. A note has three parts.

The Head: gives a general indication of time: a hollow oval indicates a half note or a whole note, while a solid oval denotes a quarter, eighth, or other note.

The Head

The Stem: all notes except for whole notes have a stem.

The Stem

The Flag: the presence of a flag indicates an eighth or sixteenth note.

The Flag

You can find notes *on* the staff, *above* the staff, and *below* the staff.

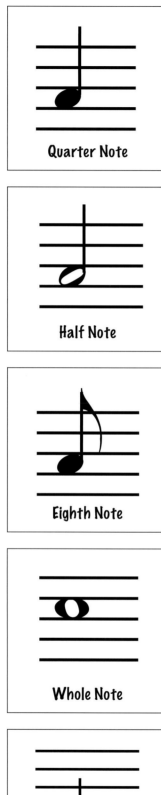

Quarter Note

Half Note

Eighth Note

Whole Note

A quarter note has a stem and a solid oval head. It usually gets one count. If there are four beats in the measure, you might count "one, two, three, four" in your mind when playing; the quarter note would generally be played for the amount of time it takes to count "one."

Notes with a stem and hollow oval head are called half notes. A half note gets two counts, or beats, per measure. It is twice as long as a quarter note, so count "one, two."

An eighth note has a solid head, a stem, and a flag. Often, two eighth notes will be connected. The eighth note lasts half as long as a quarter note. So if you are mentally counting the beats in the measure, you would count "one and two and three and four and." Each of these words would represent an eighth note; you would play on the "one" but not on the "and," for example.

A whole note is a hollow circle. It indicates a note that receives four beats.

Sometimes, you will see a dot next to a note, as shown in the lower left corner. This means that when you play the note, you need to add one-half the original value of the note to its length. For example, a dotted half note is played for three beats, while a dotted quarter note is extended by an extra eighth. (In 4/4 time each measure would have eight eighth notes; the dotted quarter note would be played for three eighths.)

Rests also appear in the measure. These symbols indicate to the musician when he or she should take a brief break from playing. Like notes, there are different symbols for rests, depending on how long the musician should be silent. Two common rests, quarter note and half note rests, are pictured below.

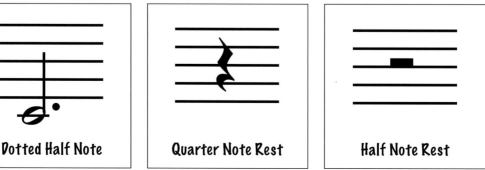

Dotted Half Note   **Quarter Note Rest**   **Half Note Rest**

3. Reading Musical Notes

Now that you have been introduced to reading music, it's time to take the next step. You have seen the staff, with its five lines and four spaces. You now need to learn the names of the lines and spaces of the staff. Here are the notes on the lines:

The note on the bottom line is E. The next line up is G, then B, then D, and finally F. Most students use a mnemonic device to remember the lines. They memorize the phrase:

Every **G**ood **B**oy **D**eserves **F**udge

The spaces from the bottom up are F, A, C, E. Yes, it's the word "face," which is another mnemonic that students can use to remember the notes in the spaces.

Music uses only the letters A through G, and the notes are always in alphabetical order. So if you start on the bottom line, E, the next space is F, the next line is G, and the following space is A. The next line will be B and so on. However, notes can also be written above and below the staff:

In the example above, some of the notes have an extra line or two through them, either above or below the five-line staff. These are called ledger lines, and they help the musician to easily identify the proper note.

4. Clef Symbols

In the previous section, specific notes were assigned to the lines and spaces on the staff. The way that you can be sure what note each line or space represents is to look at the beginning of the first staff of music. There, you will see a symbol called a clef. There are several different clef symbols; each indicates to the person reading the music which notes the lines and spaces on the staff represent. For the violin you will only need to know one, the treble, or G, clef. When you see the treble clef, you'll know that the notes on the lines are EGBDF and the notes on the spaces are FACE.

Another commonly used clef is the bass clef, but this is mostly found in piano and bass instrument music. While we won't be covering how to read bass clef in this book, it's still good to know the symbol in case you ever come across it. The lines and spaces in bass clef have different note values than the lines and spaces have in treble clef.

The Treble Clef

The Bass Clef

5. Time Signature

In addition to the clef, there is also a time signature written at the beginning of the musical staff. The time signature tells the musician how many beats are in each measure and which note is valued at one beat.

The top number indicates the number of beats per measure. So in 4/4 time, there are four beats per measure, while in 3/4 time there are three beats per measure. The bottom number tells which note gets one beat. A 4 on the bottom of the time signature means the quarter note gets one beat. In 6/8 time each measure would have 6 beats and the eighth note would be played as one beat.

Below are some examples of time signatures that are often used in violin music. You will sometimes see a C in the place of a time signature. That simply stands for 4/4, or common time. Most of the music you will see will be written either in 4/4 or 3/4 time.

2/4 Time

4/4 Time
(also known as common time)

3/4 Time   6/8 Time

6. The Sharp and Flat Signs

The figure on the F line on the staff to the right is called a sharp. If you see it placed in front of a note, you should play the note a half step up. For example, if you see an F with the # before it, you would not play F, you would play the note a half tone higher. This note is called F#.

Notes can also be flat, which means they are played a half tone lower. A flat sign looks like a small b (pictured at left). As you've probably figured out, sharps and flats can indicate the same tone. The note G is one step above F, so you use the same fingering to play F# (a half-step up) and

Gb (a half-step down). These are known as enharmonic notes.

The first place you will see flats and sharps is in the key signature. If you see one sharp in the key signature (like in the first image in this section) the music is in the key of G. If you see one flat in the key signature (as in the second image in this section), the music is in the key of F. Below are the sharps and flats that will appear in the key signatures of some other musical keys.

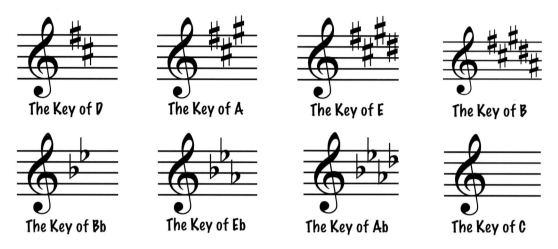

The Key of D   The Key of A   The Key of E   The Key of B

The Key of Bb   The Key of Eb   The Key of Ab   The Key of C

Sometimes a song may include a note or notes that are not in the same key as the rest of the song. When this happens, you will see a sharp or flat symbol next to the note in your music. If the note is already sharp or flat, you may see another symbol next to the note. This means to play the natural tone. Musicians call these notes "accidentals."

Natural Symbol

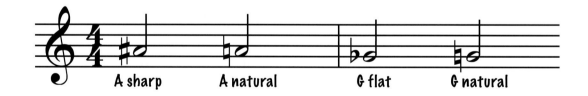

A sharp   A natural   G flat   G natural

Let's Review

1. Music is written on a **staff**, which has **five** lines and **four** spaces.
2. The notes of the lines are **EGBDF.**
3. The notes of the spaces are **FACE.**
4. Violin music is normally written in the **treble clef**.
5. The staff is divided into **measures** by vertical lines called **bar lines**.

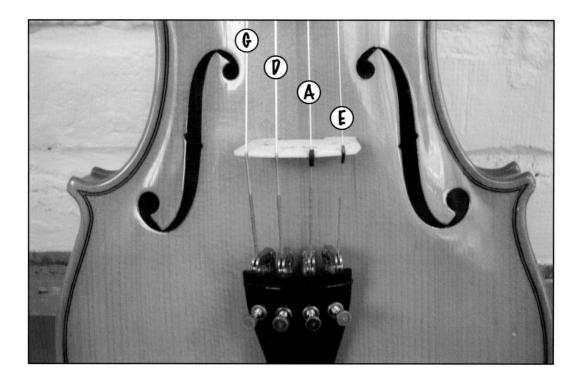

7. Tuning the Strings

Now that you know something about the notes and reading music, you are ready to tune the strings of the violin. If the strings are not properly tuned, your instrument will not sound right. Each string is supposed to play a particular note. The lowest string, which is also the thickest string, plays the note G. The next string plays the note D, followed by A, and then E, which is played on the thinnest string.

The four strings on the violin are tuned in what musicians call "perfect fifths." A fifth represents five lines and spaces, which means that each string on the violin is four notes apart from the one next to it. If you start with the lowest string, G, and count up four notes, you are on the note D. Counting up four more notes brings you to A. Four notes up from that is the note E.

To tune the violin, you will need a pitch pipe that produces the notes G, D, A, and E; you can also use a piano, if you have access to one. Violinists typically begin with the A string. Play the A on your pitch pipe or strike the A above Middle C on the piano. Then pluck the A string on the violin. If the sound of the string (the pitch) does not sound the same as the note produced by the pitch pipe or piano, gently turn the peg until the string reaches the correct pitch. Adjusting the pegs by turning them right (if the string sounds too low) or left (if the string sounds too high) should get you very close to the proper note. Use the fine tuner to match the note exactly.

Once the A string plays the correct pitch, tune the other strings. Your pitch pipe will produce the proper notes; if you're using a piano, tune the D string to the D above Middle C, the G string to the G below Middle C, and the E string to the second E above Middle C.

PART THREE: Let's Play!

1. Pizzicato

Now you're ready to start playing. But before you get the bow out, you're going to try simply plucking the strings. Place the violin under your chin as if you were going to play, then use your right hand to pluck the D string between the bridge and the fingerboard. The proper way to do this is to arch the index finger of your right hand over the string and use the tip of that finger, very near the fingernail, to pick the string. This is called playing pizzicato. You can practice this technique with the following pizzicato exercises.

Playing pizzicato, the G string

Playing pizzicato, the D string

Playing pizzicato, the A string

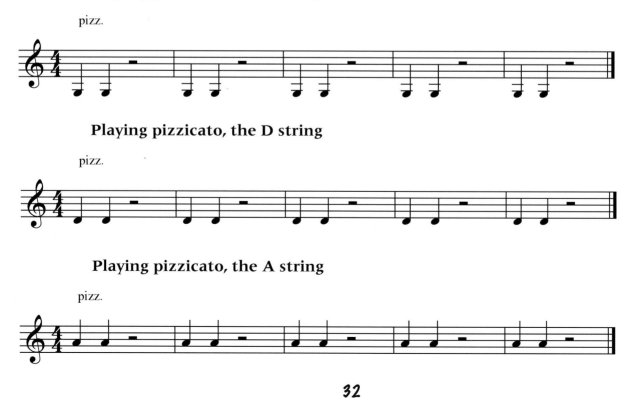

Playing pizzicato, the E string

When the "pizz." symbol appears in a piece of music, the violin player should play pizzicato until he or she see the word "arco," which means "to bow." Typically, the violin player continues to hold the bow when playing pizzicato, so that he or she is ready to return to playing notes with the bow when instructed. In some pieces where pizzicato is played for a long time, the violinist may be able to put down the bow.

It is also possible to play pizzicato with your left hand. However, this is very rare, and you might never see the symbol for left-handed pizzicato (a small cross) in your violin music. But if you do, hold the bottom of the violin with your right hand. Reach your left hand around the fingerboard of the violin, like you would to play the notes, and pluck the appropriate strings using the index finger of your left hand.

Playing pizzicato, left-handed, G, D, A, and E strings

HELPFUL TIP:
When you see the label "pizz." above your music, you'll know that you should play pizzicato with your right hand. A cross symbol means to pluck the strings with your left hand.

2. Playing with the Bow

Now you're ready to try sounding notes with the bow. Again, place the violin under your chin and pick up the bow. Make sure to hold it properly, as illustrated above.

The bow should be placed between the bridge and the fingerboard. Try to play slowly and smoothly. Only use a downward stroke for now. To play a downward stroke, place the heel of the bow on the string and draw your hand down, bringing the tip of the bow close to the string.

When you see this symbol written above your music, you should play a downstroke with the bow.

The upstroke is marked with a different symbol, shown below.

3. The D String

The first string to try is the D string. (This is the second string from the left.) The way the note will appear in your music is pictured to the right. Play the string open for now—that is, don't place a finger on the string. Draw the bow across the D string in a downstroke, being careful not to bump any of the other strings on the way.

The Note D (Open D String)

Once you're feeling comfortable and confident that you can play the note cleanly and clearly, try practicing with the following exercises. In the first one, you will be playing half notes. Remember to always check the time signature—in 4/4 time, there are four beats in each measure and half notes are held for two beats. In this exercise, you will draw the bow across the strings while you count "one, two." At that point you'll have reached the half-note rest in the music, so lift the bow off the strings and count "three, four." Lifting the bow will cause the note to stop playing.

Open D string, half notes and rests, downstrokes

In this next exercise, you will play two half notes in each measure. You need to draw the bow across the D string for a count of "one, two," then quickly lift and replace it on the string, drawing for a count of "three, four." In this exercise, you should hear two distinct notes in each measure.

Open D string, half notes, downstrokes

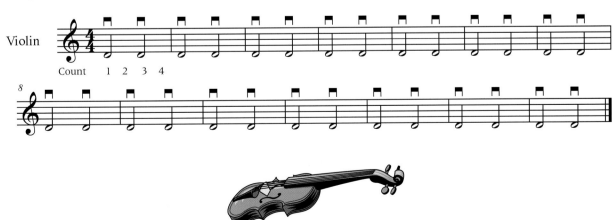

This next exercise is quarter notes, which each get one beat in 4/4 time. That means in each measure you need to play four notes—one for each beat. To do this, you'll need to use short, quick downstrokes.

Open D string, quarter notes, downstrokes

When playing whole notes in 4/4 time, the note is held for four beats. You can use a long, slow downstroke for these notes; just lift the bow at the end of each measure so that you can play the next note on the proper beat.

Open D string, whole notes and rests, downstrokes

Playing eighth notes will require you to get two notes in each beat, where they are marked. Instead of counting "one, two, three, four," try counting "one and two and three and four and," and playing notes both on the beat ("one, two," etc.) and on the "and." Here you play four eighth notes in the first two beats of each measure, and rest on the last two beats.

Open D string, eighth notes and rests, downstrokes

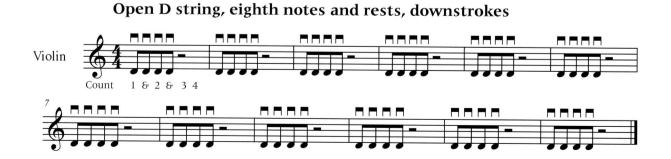

When you're feeling comfortable with the downstroke, try the following exercises. They will help you get a feel for the different notes using the upstroke.

Open D string, half notes and rests, upstrokes

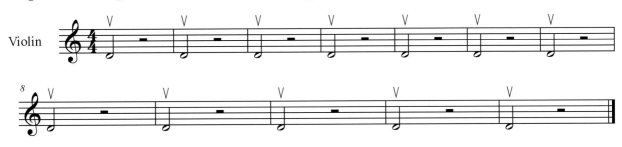

Open D string, quarter notes, upstrokes

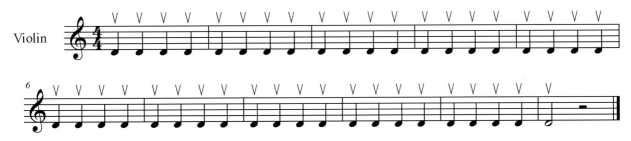

Open D string, whole notes and rests, upstrokes

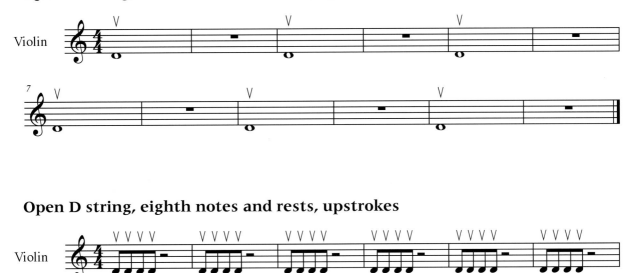

Open D string, eighth notes and rests, upstrokes

Here are some exercises that will let you practice using both downstrokes and upstrokes.

Open D string, half notes and rests, downstrokes and upstrokes, exercise 1

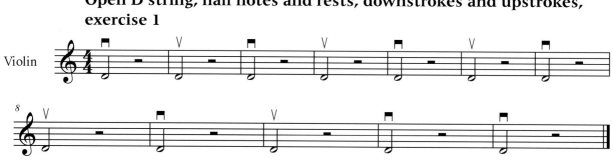

Open D string, quarter notes, downstrokes and upstrokes

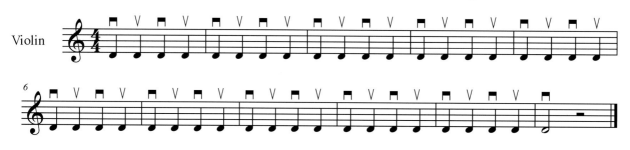

Here, you rest on beats one and two and play on beats three and four.

Open D string, half notes and rests, downstrokes and upstrokes, exercise 2

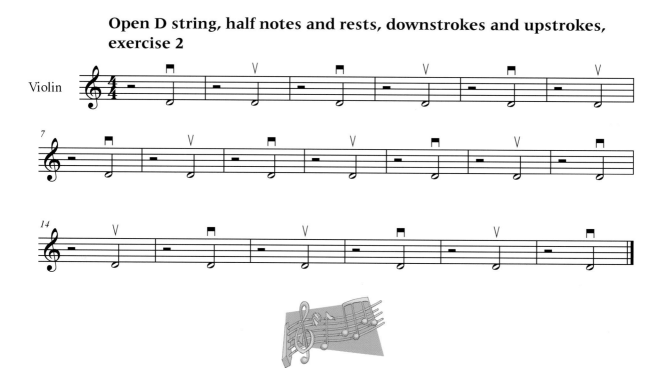

4. The A String

The next string to try playing is the A string. When you look at the violin, this is the string to the right of the D string. The note as it will appear in your music is pictured at right.

The Note A (Open A String)

One thing you may notice when you try playing the A string is that the notes may sound squeaky. This is a common problem that people who are just learning the violin have when they play higher notes. Be patient, and practice playing the string until you get a pleasing sound.

Start playing the string using downstrokes.

Open A string, half notes and rests, downstrokes

Open A string, quarter notes, downstrokes

Open A string, whole notes and rests, downstrokes

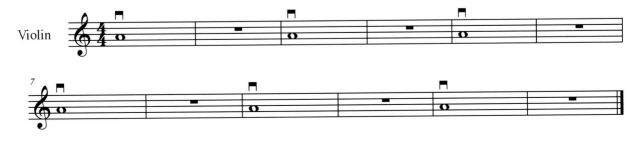

Open A string, eighth notes and rests, downstrokes

Now try a few lessons using upstrokes.

Open A string, half notes and rests, upstrokes

Open A string, half notes, upstrokes

Open A string, quarter notes, upstrokes

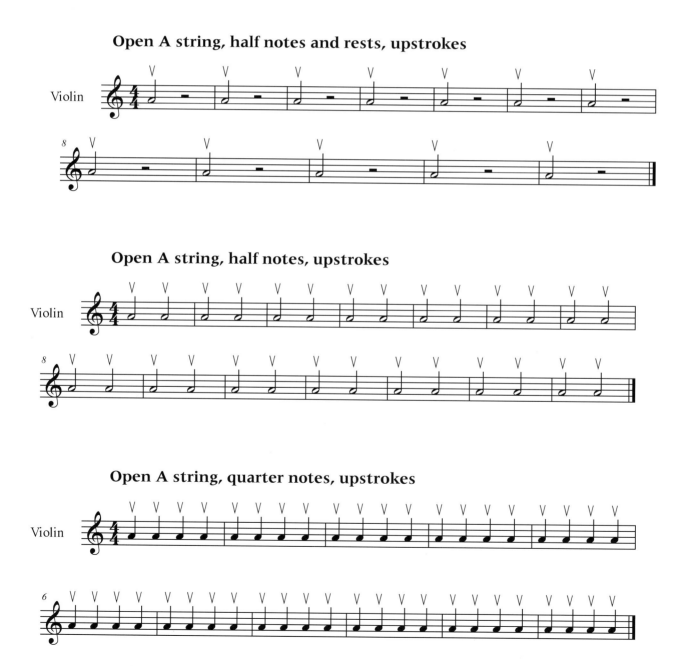

Open A string, whole notes and rests, upstrokes

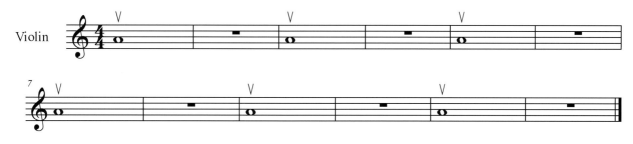

Open A string, eighth notes and rests, upstrokes

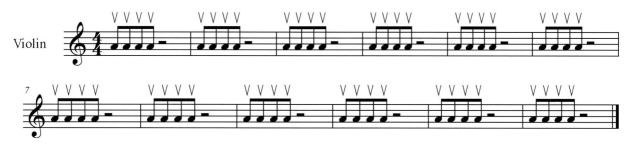

Combining downstrokes and upstrokes is a crucial skill. Practice these lessons slowly and carefully.

Open A string, half notes and rests, downstrokes and upstrokes, exercise 1

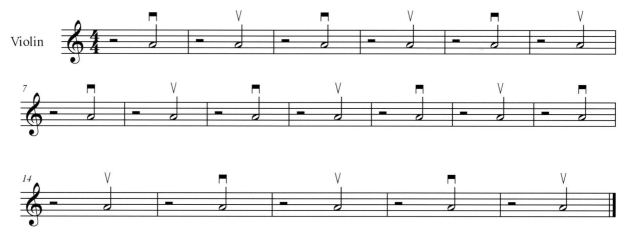

Open A string, quarter notes, half notes, and rests, downstrokes and upstrokes, exercise 1

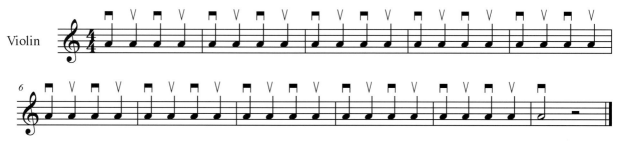

Open A string, whole notes and rests, downstrokes and upstrokes, exercise 1

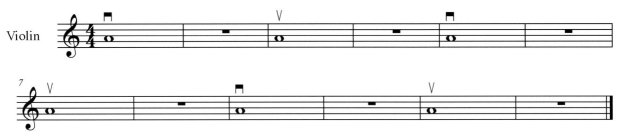

Open A string, eighth notes and rests, downstrokes and upstrokes, exercise 1

Open A string, quarter notes and rests, downstrokes and upstrokes, exercise 2

Open A string, whole notes and rests, downstrokes and upstrokes, exercise 2

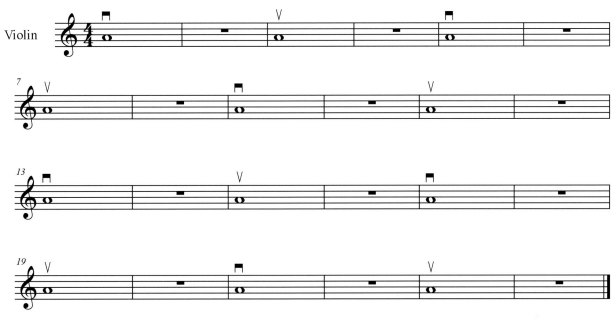

Open A string, eighth notes and rests, downstrokes and upstrokes, exercise 2

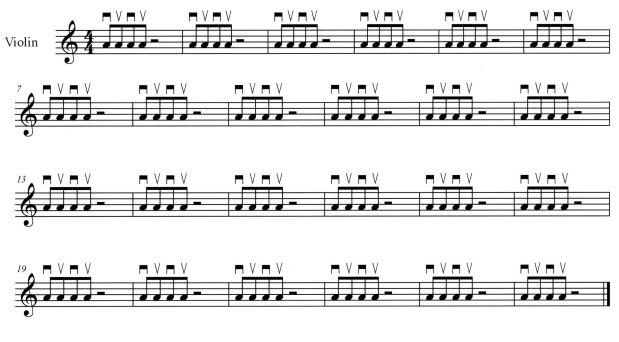

5. Playing the D and A Strings

Now, try playing two notes, going back and forth between the A and D strings. You'll notice that playing the different strings will require you to angle your arm and wrist differently.

Open D and A strings, half notes and rests, and quarter notes, downstrokes

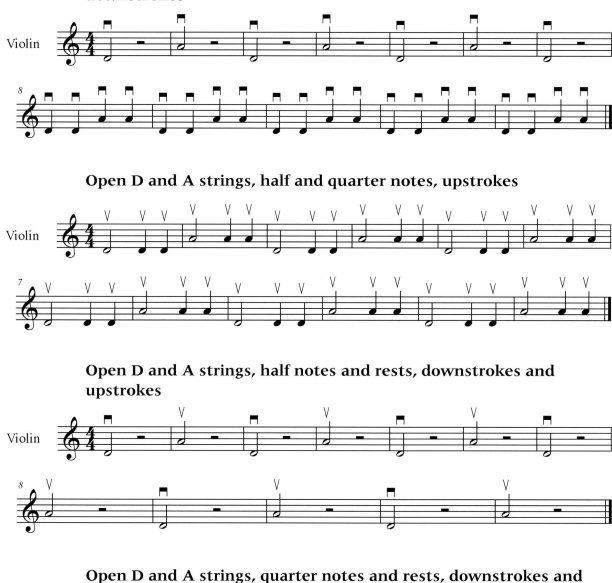

Open D and A strings, half and quarter notes, upstrokes

Open D and A strings, half notes and rests, downstrokes and upstrokes

Open D and A strings, quarter notes and rests, downstrokes and upstrokes

**Open D and A strings, whole notes and rests,
downstrokes and upstrokes**

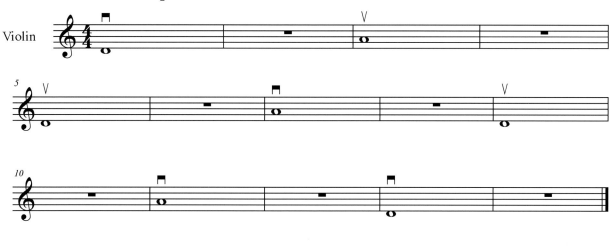

**Open D and A strings, eighth notes and rests,
downstrokes and upstrokes**

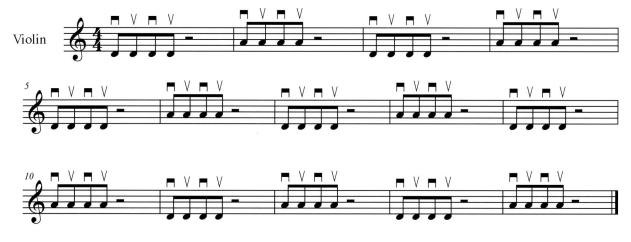

**Open D and A strings, half notes, quarter notes, and rests,
downstrokes and upstrokes**

6. The G String

Let's move on to the lowest string on the violin, the G string. This is the string all the way to the left. You'll probably find that you have to lift your hand high in order to play the G string.

The Note G (Open G String)

Open G string, half notes and rests, downstrokes

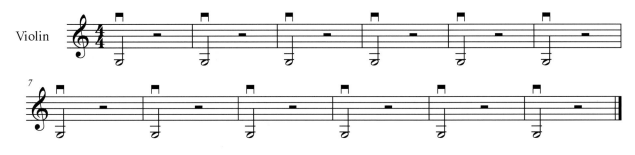

Open G string, quarter notes, downstrokes

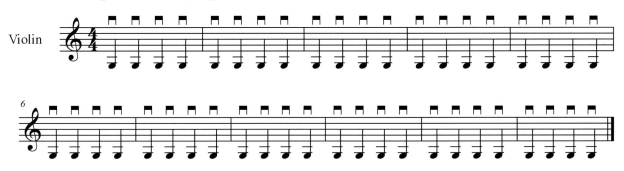

HELPFUL TIP:
Remember to be aware of your posture as you play. One way to do this is to practice in front of a mirror.

Open G string, whole notes and rests, downstrokes

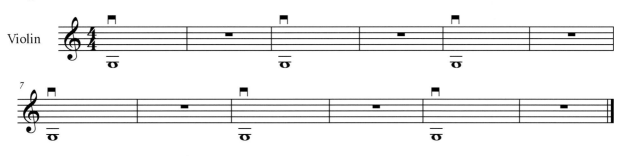

Open G string, eighth notes and rests, downstrokes

Open G string, half notes and rests, upstrokes

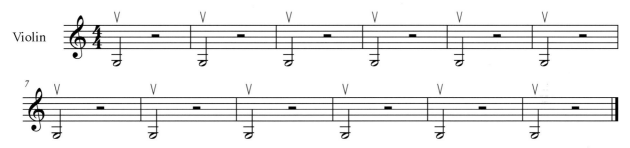

Open G string, half notes, upstrokes

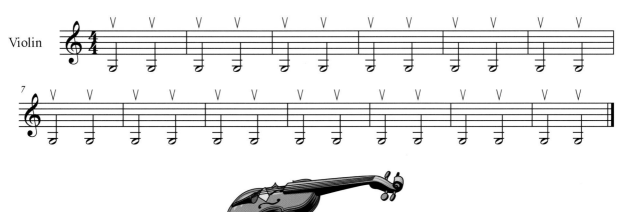

Open G string, quarter notes, half notes, and rests, upstrokes

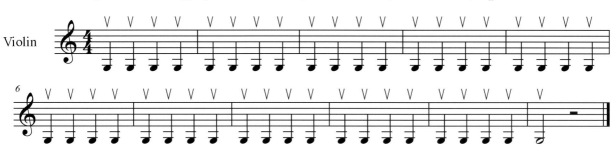

Open G string, whole notes and rests, upstrokes

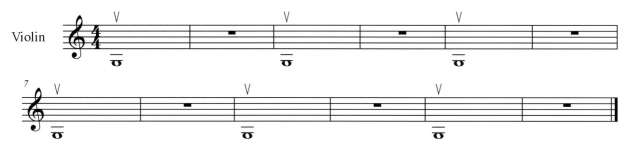

Open G string, eighth notes and rests, upstrokes

7. G String Downstroke and Upstroke Exercises

Practice the next set of exercises to work on bowing both downstrokes and upstrokes.

Open G string, half notes and rests, downstrokes and upstrokes, exercise 1

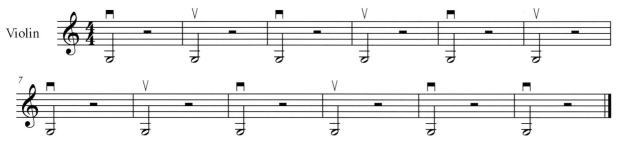

Open G string, half notes, downstrokes and upstrokes, exercise 2

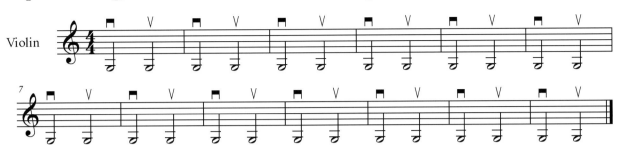

Open G string, half notes and rests, downstrokes and upstrokes, exercise 3

Open G string, quarter notes, downstrokes and upstrokes

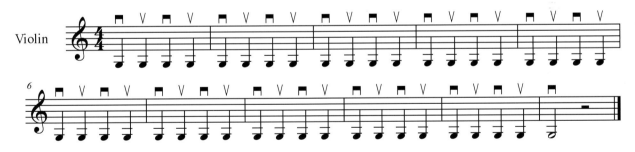

Open G string, whole notes and rests, downstrokes and upstrokes

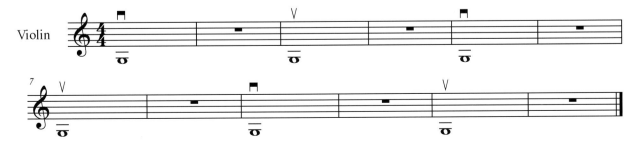

8. The E String

The E string is the highest string on the violin. Remember, high notes on a violin have a tendency to be squeaky, so you may have to practice playing this string a lot before you can produce a pleasant tone.

The Note E (Open E String)

Open E string, eighth notes and rests, downstrokes

Open E string, half notes and rests, upstrokes

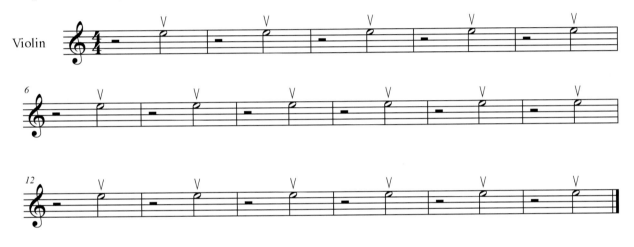

Open E string, quarter notes and rests, upstrokes

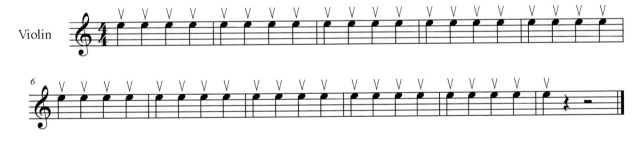

Open E string, whole notes and rests, upstrokes

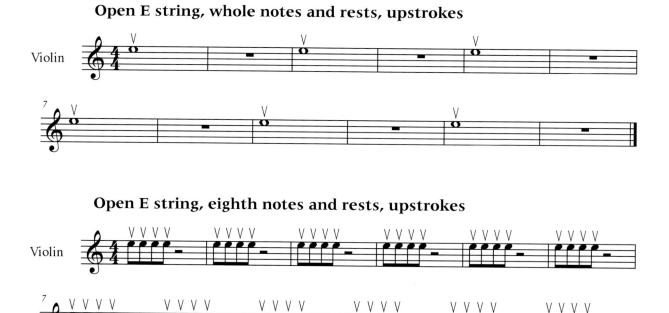

Open E string, eighth notes and rests, upstrokes

9. E String Downstroke and Upstroke Exercises

By now you should be familiar with the notation for downstrokes and upstrokes. Stay alert to make sure you are playing the exercises properly.

Open E string, half notes and rests, downstrokes and upstrokes

Open E string, quarter notes, half notes, and rests, downstrokes and upstrokes

Open E string, whole notes and rests, downstrokes and upstrokes

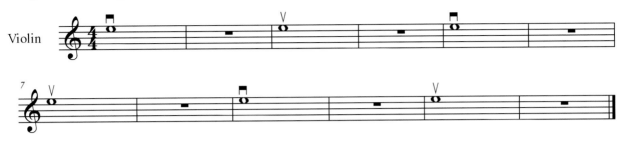

10. Switching Between Strings

Now you're ready to try playing all the open strings together. Switching between strings will require you to move your entire right arm. Imagine your arm as being weightless, existing only so that your hand can move to where it needs to be. If you need to reach the G string, your hand should float up until contact is made. If you're playing the E string, it should dip down, bringing the whole arm with it. Try to keep the bow at a right angle to the strings. Play slow and steady at first, then pick up the tempo.

Half notes and rests on all strings, downstrokes

Half notes and rests on all strings, upstrokes

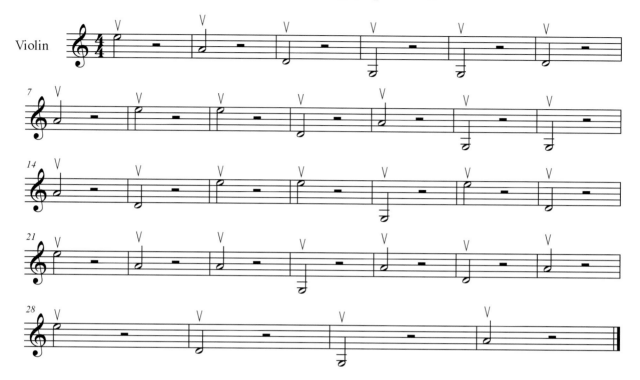

Half notes and rests on all strings, downstrokes and upstrokes, exercise 1

Half notes and rests on all strings, downstrokes and upstrokes, exercise 2

Half notes, quarter notes, and rests on all strings, downstrokes and upstrokes, exercise 1

Half notes, quarter notes, and rests on all strings, downstrokes and upstrokes, exercise 2

Quarter notes and half notes on all strings, downstrokes and upstrokes

11. Playing Notes that Require Fingering

Up to this point you have been playing only on the open strings. This has allowed you to develop a feel for how to balance the instrument and hold the bow. By this point, you should also have a better understanding of what correctly played violin notes sound like. It is essential for violin players to develop a "musician's ear"—a sense of whether notes sound right or wrong, You must be able to tell when a note is off-key or whether it is being played properly.

To play notes that require fingering, you first need to know how those notes should sound. This means you must use something other than your violin to produce the notes. Ideally, a properly tuned piano will enable you to find any note you need. However, if you do not have a piano, you could also use tuning forks or pitch pipes to produce certain notes. You might also try finding a program for your computer that will play notes—search the Internet for a free synthesizer program. (One program can be found at http://www.download.com/Click-MusicalKeys/3000-2133_4-10452010 .html?tag=lst-0-1)

12. The Note E Above Middle C

The first fingered note you will learn how to play is the E above Middle C. First, play that note several times on your reference source (piano, tuning fork, pitch pipe, computer, etc.) so that you know exactly how it should sound.

To find the note E above Middle C on your violin, start by playing the open D string. Then press the tip of your left index finger (this will be called finger 1) onto the string, and shift it up and down until the note coming from your violin exactly matches the note you heard on your piano or other reference source. (When you play the E above Middle C, you'll notice that it sounds like a lower version of the note pro-

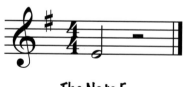

The Note E

duced by playing the open E string. This is because it is the same note, just an octave lower.)

Because the fingerboard of the violin has no markings, it is difficult for a beginning violin player to hit the same spot each time he or she wants to play a fingered note. One way to help you learn the proper spot is to mark it with a small piece of white tape, or a dot of liquid correction fluid. The more you practice the note, however, the deeper the action of playing it will become ingrained in your wrist, arm, fingers, and mind. Eventually, you'll find that you can remove all of the helpful guides and learn to play by feel alone.

The photos on the opposite page show the approximate fingering of the E above Middle C.

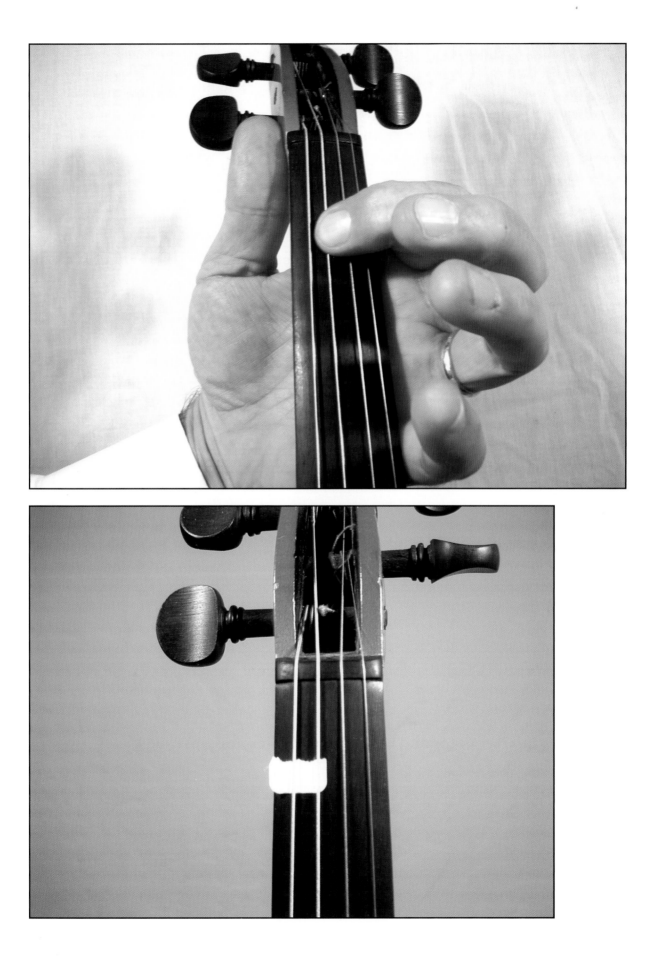

13. E Above Middle C Exercises

Let's try some exercises with the new note. First, just play the E.

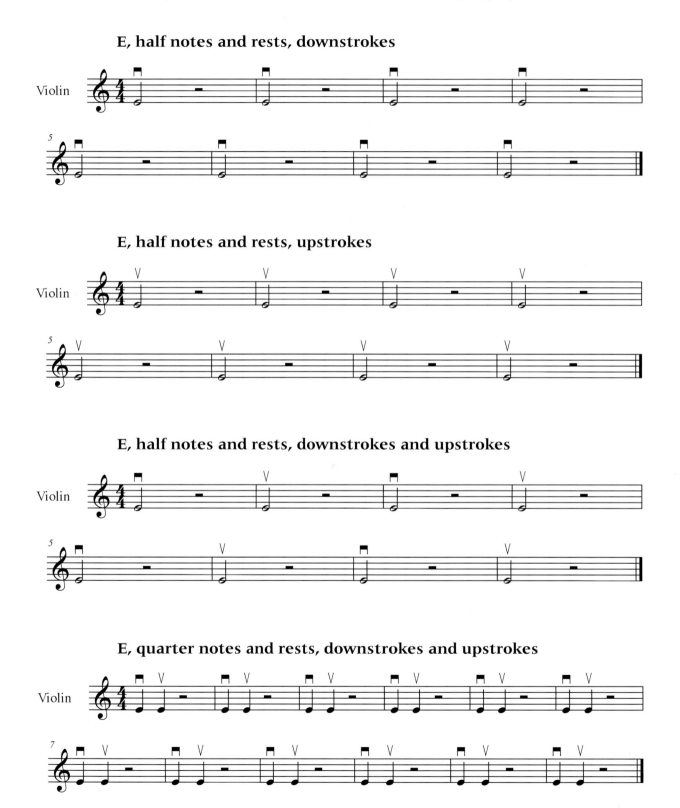

E, half notes and rests, downstrokes

E, half notes and rests, upstrokes

E, half notes and rests, downstrokes and upstrokes

E, quarter notes and rests, downstrokes and upstrokes

E, whole notes and rests, downstrokes and upstrokes

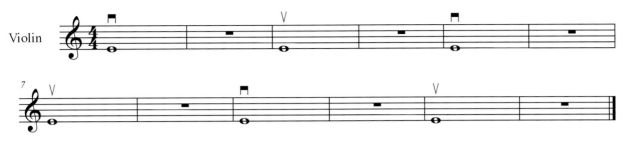

E, eighth notes and rests, downstrokes and upstrokes

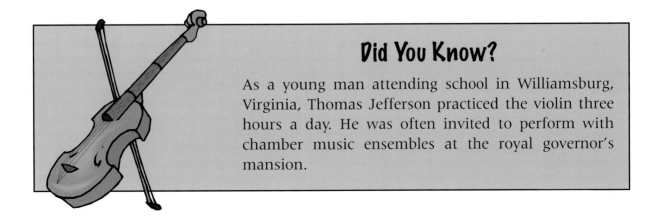

Did You Know?

As a young man attending school in Williamsburg, Virginia, Thomas Jefferson practiced the violin three hours a day. He was often invited to perform with chamber music ensembles at the royal governor's mansion.

14. Playing the Notes You Know, Downstrokes

Now try switching from note to note. This is a difficult skill to learn, so there are many lessons in this section. First try using only downstrokes. Switching between strings, and between open and fingered notes, takes a lot of practice, so be patient and take your time on each exercise. Practice until you are confident before moving on to the next section.

A to E, half notes and rests, downstrokes

E to A, half notes and rests, downstrokes

A to E, quarter notes and rests, downstrokes

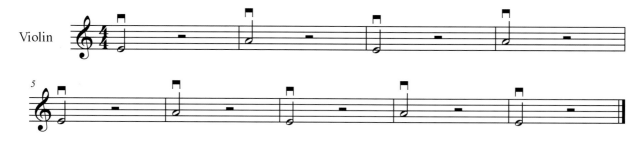

E to A, quarter notes and rests, downstrokes

D to E, half notes and rests, downstrokes

E to D, half notes and rests, downstrokes

D to E, quarter notes and rests, downstrokes

E to D, quarter notes and rests, downstrokes

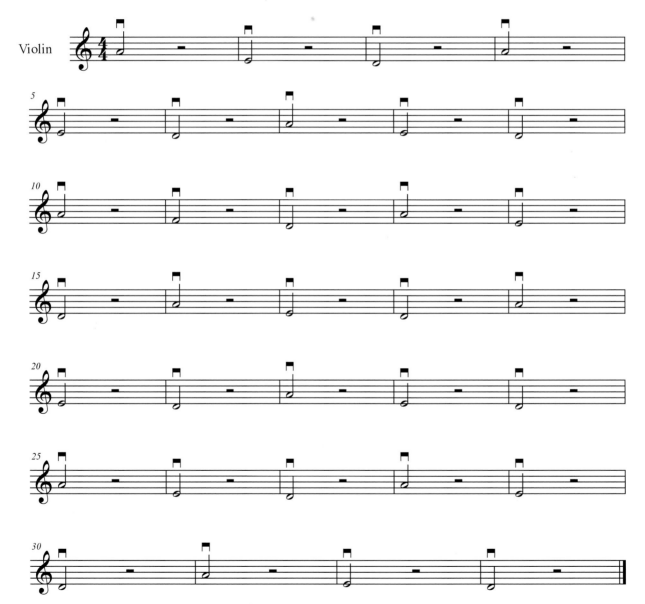

A to E to D, half notes and rests, downstrokes

D to E to A, half notes and rests, downstrokes

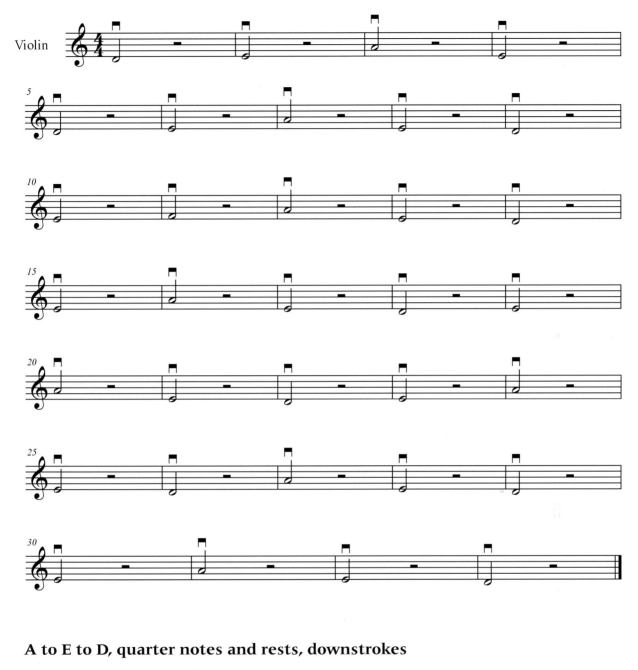

A to E to D, quarter notes and rests, downstrokes

A to E, quarter notes and rests, downstrokes

15. Playing the Notes You Know, Upstrokes

Now attempt to play using upstrokes. Proceed slowly and try to make sure the notes are as clear as possible. The most important part of these exercises is finding E. You want the fingering for E to become an automatic movement, so your index finger finds the note without your having to look.

A to E, half notes and rests, upstrokes

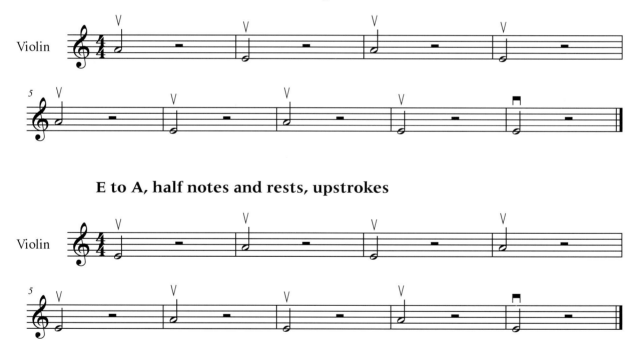

E to A, half notes and rests, upstrokes

A to E, quarter notes and rests, upstrokes

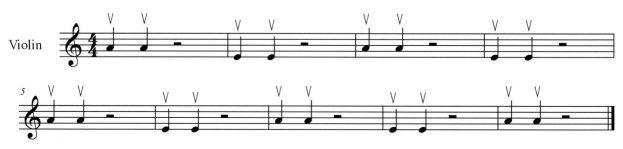

E to A, quarter notes and rests, upstrokes

D to E, half notes and rests, upstrokes

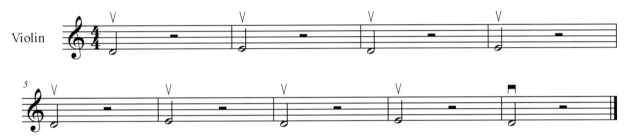

E to D, half notes and rests, upstrokes

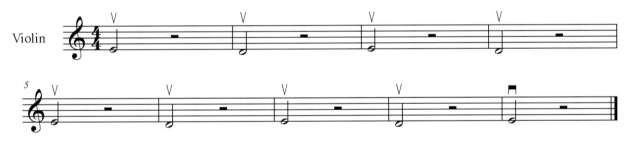

D to E, quarter notes and rests, upstrokes

E to D, quarter notes and rests, upstrokes

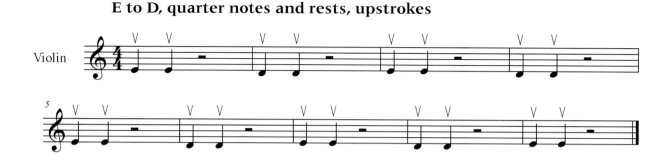

D to E to A, half notes and rests, upstrokes

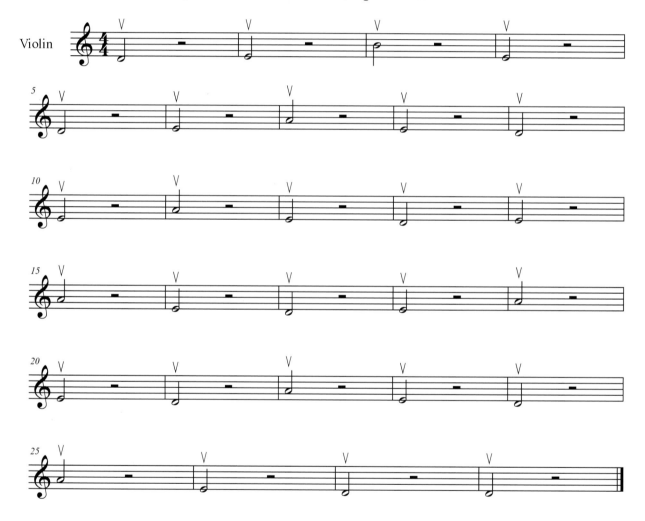

D to E to A, quarter notes and rests, upstrokes

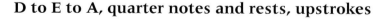

D to E to A, half notes and rests, upstrokes

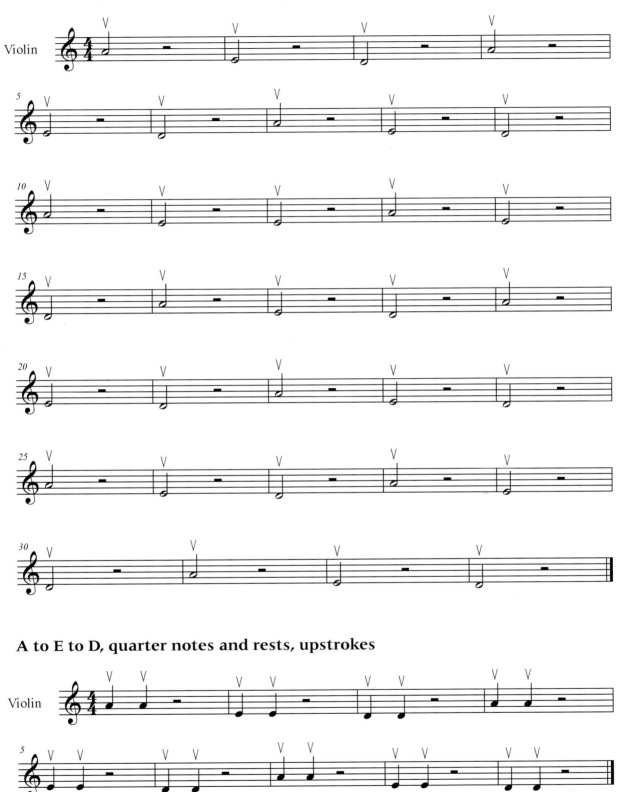

A to E to D, quarter notes and rests, upstrokes

16. Downstroke and Upstroke Exercises

Now you're ready to practice bowing with downstrokes and upstrokes as well as switching between open and fingered notes. By now, you may be able to find the E without looking at the mark on the fingerboard. If you think you're ready, remove the mark and practice the following exercises without a guide.

A to E, half notes and rests, downstrokes and upstrokes

E to A, half notes and rests, downstrokes and upstrokes

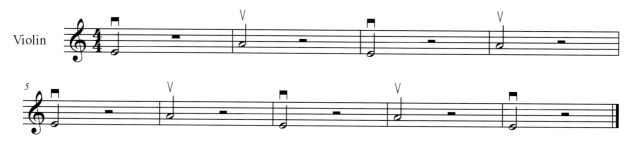

A to E, quarter notes and rests, downstrokes and upstrokes

E to A, quarter notes and rests, downstrokes and upstrokes

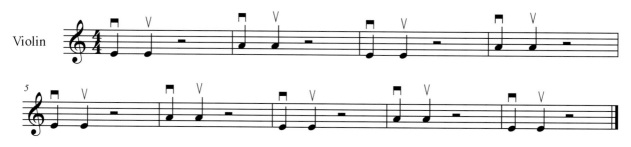

D to E, half notes and rests, downstrokes and upstrokes

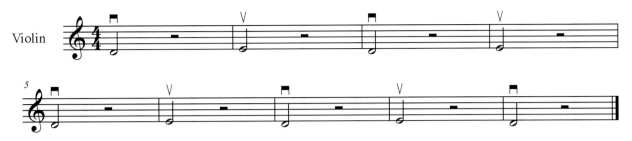

E to D, half notes and rests, downstrokes and upstrokes

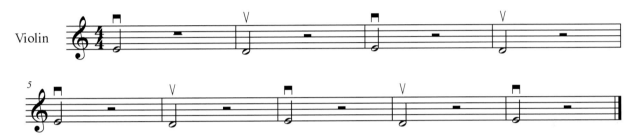

D to E, quarter notes and rests, downstrokes and upstrokes

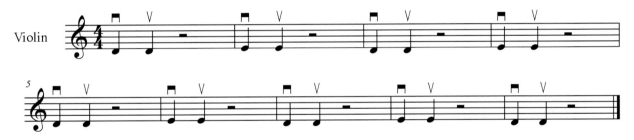

E to D, quarter notes and rests, downstrokes and upstrokes

A to E to D, quarter notes and rests, downstrokes and upstrokes

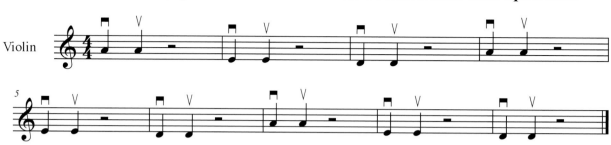

A to E to D, half notes, quarter notes, and rests, downstrokes and upstrokes

D to E to A, quarter notes and rests, downstrokes and upstrokes

D to E to A, half notes, quarter notes, and rests, downstrokes and upstrokes

17. The Note F#

Up to this point, you have been playing in the key of C. (As you may recall from pages 29–30, there are no sharp or flat notes in the key of C.) The next note you will learn is F#, which will allow you to play in the key of G.

Like the E above Middle C, the F# is played on the D string. First find F# on the piano or other tuning device and play it. Next, bow the D string and slide the middle finger of your left hand (finger 2) until you find the same note. Mark this spot with another piece of tape.

The Note F#

18. F# Exercises

Here are some exercises you can use to practice playing the note F#. Because they are written in the key of G, as indicated by the single sharp sign in the key signature, there won't be a sharp sign in front of the F in the musical staff. (Always remember to read the key signature before you start playing, so that you know which notes you should play.)

F#, half notes and rests, downstrokes

F#, half notes and rests, upstrokes

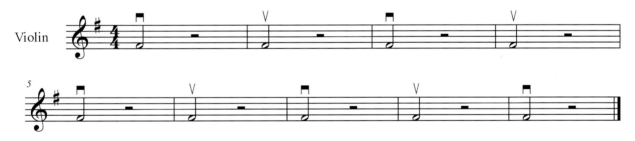

F#, half notes and rests, downstrokes and upstrokes, exercise 1

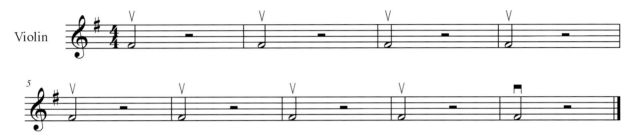

F#, half notes and rests, downstrokes and upstrokes, exercise 2

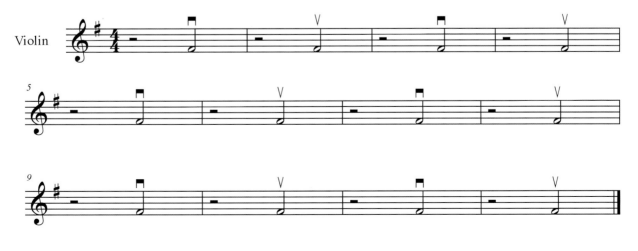

Next, try playing F# with the other notes you've learned. Practice these exercises slowly. You have to learn where F# and E are based on feel and sound alone, so you'll want to play these notes often to properly tune your ear. The fingerings are very close to one another, and you don't want to be playing a note in the middle.

Key of G, half notes, quarter notes, and rests, downstrokes and upstrokes

Key of G, half notes, eighth notes, and rests, downstrokes and upstrokes

Did You Know?

The violin is the smallest of a group of instruments known as the violin family. Other instruments in the violin family include the viola, cello, and double bass. All of these instruments traditionally have wooden bodies and f-shaped resonance holes.

19. The Note G Above Middle C and Exercises

The note G is also found on the D string. Find G on your tuning device and match it on the violin using your ring finger (finger 3). Mark this spot on the fingerboard.

Use the exercises below to practice this new note.

The Note G

G above Middle C, half notes and rests, downstrokes

G above Middle C, half notes and rests, upstrokes

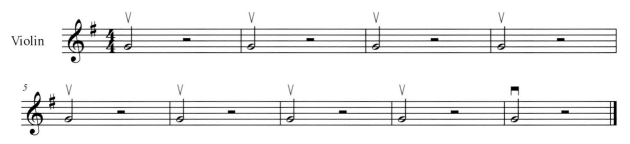

G above Middle C, half notes and rests, downstrokes and upstrokes

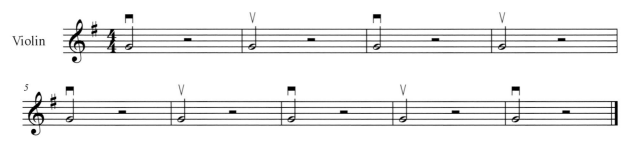

Now practice switching between the notes G and F#. These notes are found close together on the D string, but remember that you should be playing G with finger 3 and F# with finger 2.

G and F#, half notes and rests, downstrokes and upstrokes

G and F#, quarter notes and rests, downstrokes and upstrokes

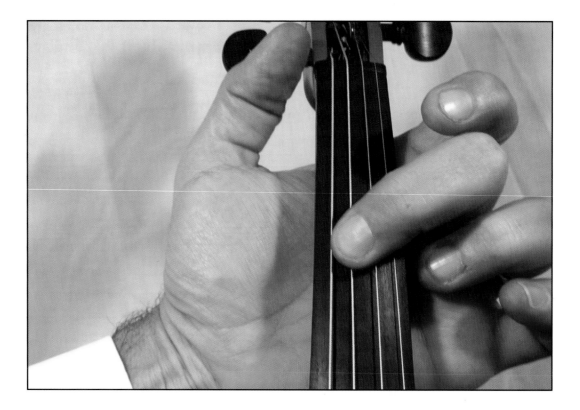

20. The Note F

The last note you will learn in this book is the note F. The addition of this note will let you move on to what you really want to do: play songs!

As with the other fingered notes, first find the note F on your tuning device. Once you know how it sounds, play the open D string and work the tip of the middle finger of your left hand up and down the string, until you find the right spot. (This note will be near F#.) Mark this note with a dot on the fingerboard.

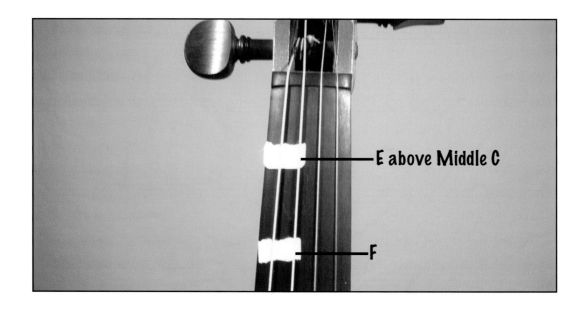

E above Middle C

F

21. F Exercises

Here are some exercises you can use to practice playing the note F.

F, half notes and rests, downstrokes

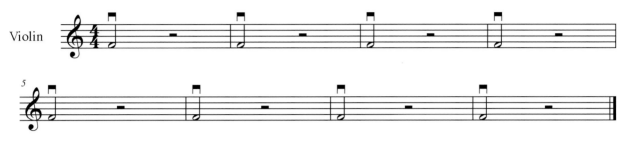

F, half notes and rests, upstrokes

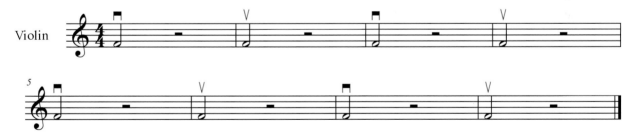

F, half notes and rests, downstrokes and upstrokes, exercise 1

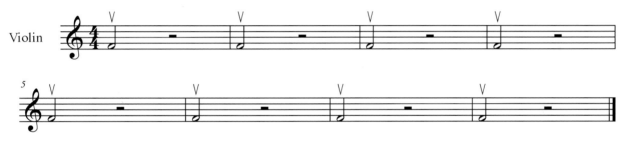

F, half notes and rests, downstrokes and upstrokes, exercise 2

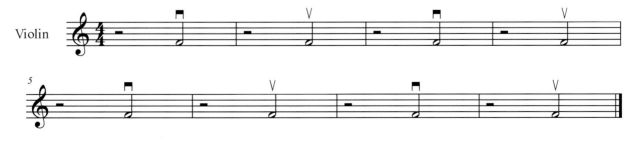

In the following exercises, pay attention to the key signatures. Some are in the key of C, and others are in G.

G through F, half notes and rests, upstrokes

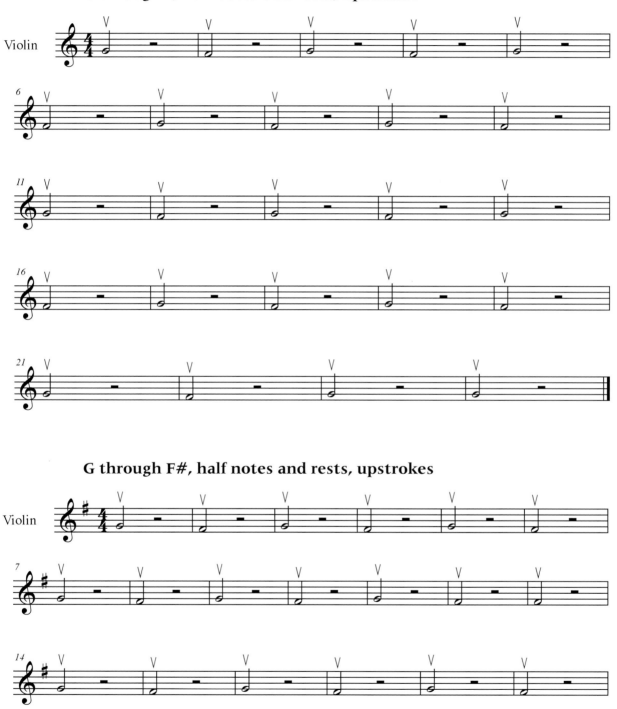

G through F#, half notes and rests, upstrokes

G through F#, half notes and rests, downstrokes

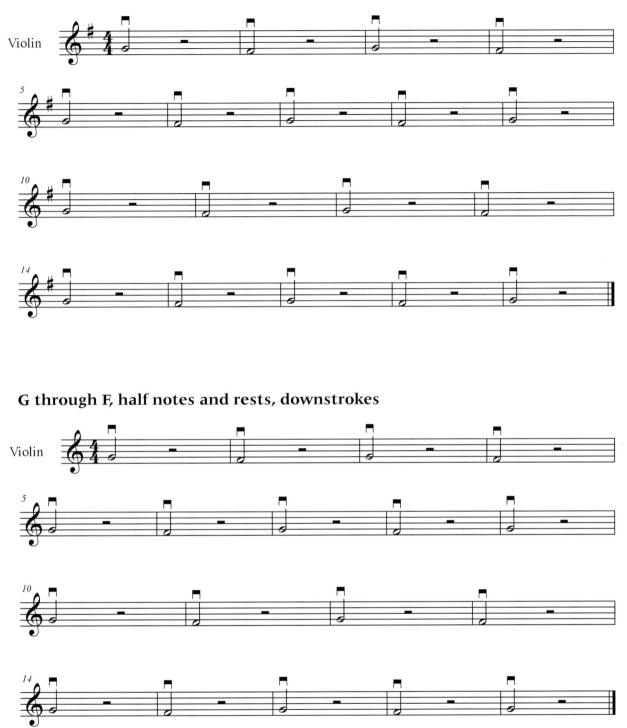

G through F, half notes and rests, downstrokes

With the exercises that follow, you will practice most of the notes you've learned so far. Once you've mastered them, you'll be ready to play the songs included in the next chapter.

G through F, quarter notes, downstrokes and upstrokes

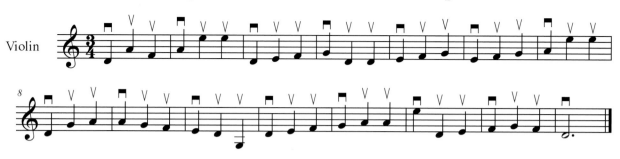

G through F, half notes, quarter notes, and rests, downstrokes and upstrokes

All open strings, half notes and rests, downstrokes and upstrokes

G through F, half notes, eighth notes, and rests, downstrokes and upstrokes

G through F, eighth notes and rests, downstrokes and upstrokes, exercise 1

G through F, eighth notes and rests, downstrokes

PART FOUR:

Songs

The following songs make use of all of the notes you've learned. You may be familiar with some of them and not familiar with others, but give them all a try.

Dog, Come Home

Traditional

Polly Wolly Doodle

Ameican

Violin

Oh, I went down south for to see my Sal, sing
Pol - ly wol - ly doo - dle all the day. My ___ Sal she is a
spunk - y gal, sing Pol - ly wol - ly doo - dle all the day. Fare thee well, fare thee
well, fare - thee well my fair - y fay, for I'm goin to Loui si an a for to
see my Su sy an na, sing Pol - ly wol ly doo dle all the day.

Did You Know?

A string quartet is one of the most common chamber music ensembles in Western music. It usually consists of two violins, a viola, and a cello. The first violin typically plays melody notes, while the second violin plays lower notes in harmony with the other instruments.

Old MacDonald Had a Farm

All the Time I Have to Spend

American

All the time I have, Lord. All the time I have to spend, Oh Lord. All the souls that must be saved, Oh Lord. All the time I have to spend sing ing to the Lord.

Walking Lightly

Spiritual

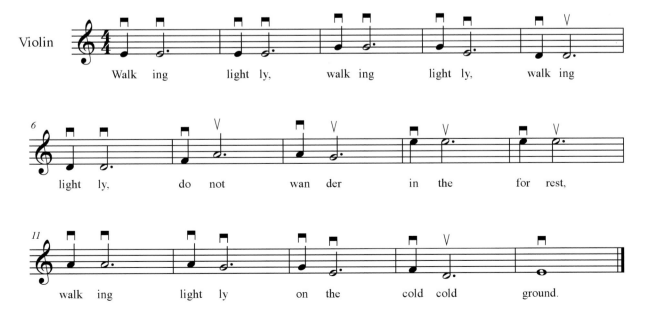

Walk ing light ly, walk ing light ly, walk ing light ly, do not wan der in the for rest, walk ing light ly on the cold cold ground.

Moonlight

Scotland

Violin

I walk with you all through the grave yard, moon light lights the way. The

moon light lights the way. Please be still and hold my hand, walk ing through the

grave yard, grave yard to night. Walk ing in the moon light, the moon will light the dark

ness. I walk with you this night, in the moon light, the

moon light. Walk with me to get her in the moon light.

Good King Toad

Traditional European

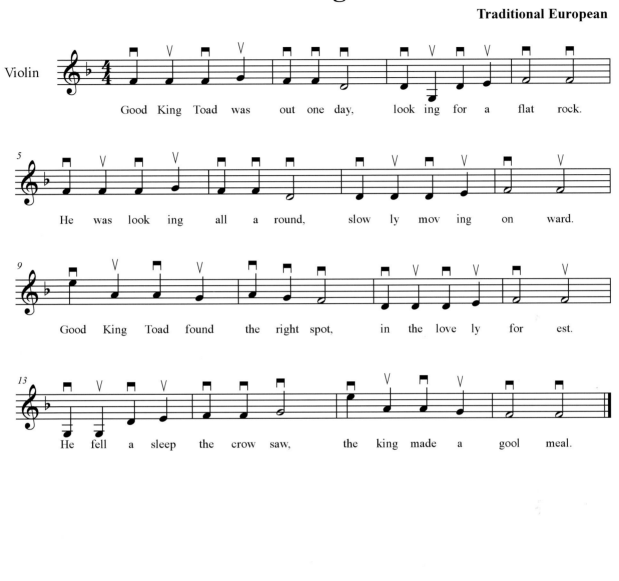

Just In Time

Welsh

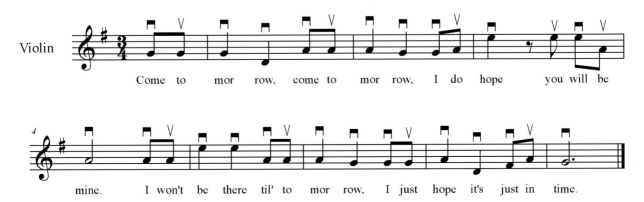

Pat-a-Pan

French Carol

Over the Hillside

Traditional English

Hometown Dances

Irish

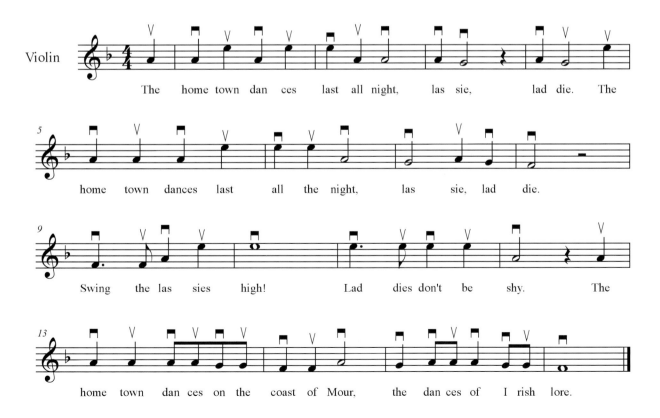

Violin

The home town dan ces last all night, las sie, lad die. The

home town dances last all the night, las sie, lad die.

Swing the las sies high! Lad dies don't be shy. The

home town dan ces on the coast of Mour, the dan ces of I rish lore.

The Waters of Maine

English Traditional

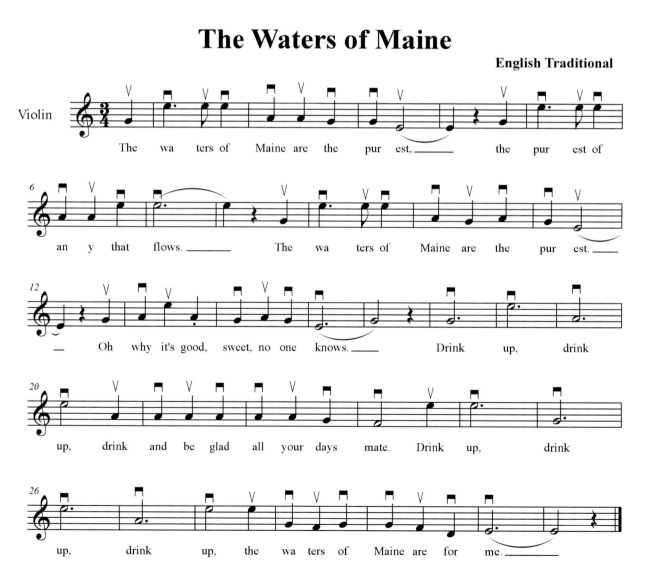

Violin

The wa ters of Maine are the pur est, _____ the pur est of

an y that flows. _____ The wa ters of Maine are the pur est. _____

_ Oh why it's good, sweet, no one knows. _____ Drink up, drink

up, drink and be glad all your days mate. Drink up, drink

up, drink up, the wa ters of Maine are for me. _____

The Bear in the Kitchen

American folk song

Violin

The bear in the kit chen, he won't go a way.

Hey, the bear in my kit chen, don't want you to stay.

Bear in the kit chen, he won't go a way.

Hey, the bear in my kit chen, don't want you to stay.

Did You Know?

A luthier is someone who makes violins and other stringed instruments. The most famous violin maker is Antonio Stradivari (1644-1737). His instruments are highly prized for their quality and are still played by professional musicians today.

It is a Time of Merriment

English Carol

Violin

It is a time of mer ri ment, the night flows in to day. It

is a time of mer ri ment, the chim ney sweeps all say, to have a drink and

kiss the las sies all a long the bay. The las sies they will drink and sing a

long. Drink ing and song, drink and song, it is a time of mer ri ment.

Did You Know?

In May 2006, a bidder paid more than $3.5 million for a Stradivarius violin named "The Hammer" at a public auction held by Christie's. Previously, the highest price ever paid for a violin was just over $2 million for another Stradivarius, the "Lady Tennant" in 2005.

Old Time Dinner

Western

Violin

I can not wait to get to Car son, I'm just tired and real ly hun gry.

An old time din ner is for me. The Car son Ciy Gold Hot el, it's the best, on ly in the

west I'l eat. An old time din ner my friend, the Gold Hot el is where I'm bound and where I'll end.

A photo of the business district in a frontier town near Carson City, Nevada, circa 1905.

Grand Olde Sea

American

Lanny and Linda

English

Violin

Lan ny and Lin da, the sis ters of Erin been

drink ing all eve ning, don't let them in.

Lan ny and Lin da, no one knows where they've been

drink ing all eve ning, don't let them in.

Did You Know?

Joseph Hayden (1732–1809) is sometimes called "father of the string quartet," as he was the first to write pieces for that ensemble. During the 1780s he occasionally performed in string quartets with his good friend, the great composer, Wolfgang Mozart.

Lullaby

World Folk Song

Violin

It's a si lent night up on us, cold and wind y it will be.

Gat her 'round the fi re burn ing while the stars a bove do shine.

God will be with you this eve ing, watch ing ov er all this night.

It's a si lent night up on us, cold and wind y it will be.

APPENDIX: Finding the Notes

Regardless of which instrument a student of music is learning, a diagram of the keys of the piano offers one of the best illustrations of how most western music is organized. Comprehending the relationship between different notes gives a violinist both a greater understanding of his or her instrument and a grasp of the basics of music theory.

Typically, a modern piano has around 88 keys. As you can see in the diagram on the opposite page, these keys are colored either black or white and repeat a specific pattern throughout the keyboard. That is, with the exception of the extreme left of the keyboard (the lowest notes) and the extreme right (the highest notes), you will find groupings of three white keys with two black keys between them and four white keys with three black keys between them. Each of these keys is given a name corresponding to the letters of the alphabet A through G. The letter names are assigned to the white, and the black keys' names are letters with either a sharp sign or flat sign after them.

The pitch that sounds when you strike the white key immediately to the left of the grouping of two black keys is known as C. Depending upon the number of keys on the piano being played, this note will reoccur six or seven times throughout the instrument. The frequency of each C is twice that of the C immediately to its left and one-half that of the C to its right. Because of this special relationship, these notes sound very similar to our ears, hence, the reason why they have the same name. The interval between these adjacent pitches with the same name is known as an octave, and this relationship is true for all similarly named notes found on the keyboard.

In order to clear up confusion caused by the fact that there are as many as 88 notes (maybe more) on a piano and many fewer note names, musicians, over time, have developed a way to differentiate between the notes that have the same name. Beginning with the C note found farthest to the left of the keyboard, a number is added to the note name indicating the octave in which the note occurs. For example, the first C that appears on the

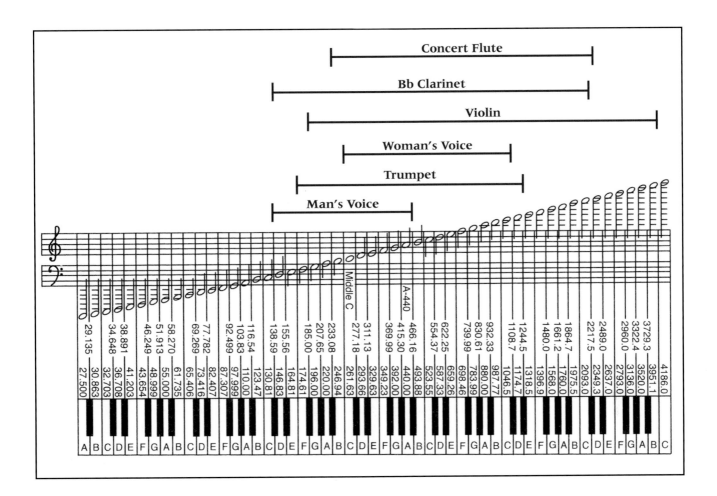

keyboard is known as "C1," the D that appears next to that is known as "D1," and so on. Middle C is also known as C4. Depending upon the piano's manufacturer, you may find that there is a different number of notes to the left of the first C on the keyboard. Since these notes do not comprise a complete octave, the number zero follows their letter name.

You'll notice that there are eleven keys between notes of the same name. Each of these keys represents a change in pitch of one half step. It can then be concluded that an octave covers a distance of 12 half steps, or six whole steps.

VIOLIN TIMELINE

A.D. 800s Early bowed string instruments begin to appear in Europe. Most probably originated in Asia or were brought by the Nordic tribes of Scandinavia.

1450s Some players of the *vihuela*, a Spanish precursor to the guitar, begin playing their instruments using bows. These instruments have frets and are referred to as the *vihuela de arco* (the word *arco* means "bow"). Because they are relatively large, they are played between the legs, leading Italian musicians to call the instruments *viola de gamba*, ("viol of the leg"), a name that helped differentiate them from a smaller instrument known as *viola da braccio* ("viol of the arm"). Also around this time, viols begin to be made with wider and higher arched bridges to make bowing single strings easier.

1500s The first violins appear in northern Italy around the turn of the century. Between 1520 and 1550, the instrument evolves into its classic form, although the number of strings continues to vary until around 1555, when Andrea Amati begins constructing violins with four strings.

1560 France's King Charles IX orders 24 violins from Amati. The world's oldest surviving violin is from this set of instruments.

1680 Antonio Stradivari opens his shop in Cremona, Italy. His instruments are considered among the finest ever made, and about 650 exist today. Some are still used by musicians.

1700s Many important changes to the construction of the violin are made, including adjustments to the length and angle of the neck. This period is considered the apogee of violin making. The Cremona "school" of luthiers leads the way, although craftsmen in Paris, London, Prague, Rome, and Mittenwald, Germany, produce excellent instruments.

1790	Dider Nicolas opens the first violin factory in Mirecourt, France. Over the next 50 years, the overall quality of violin making declines due to industrialization.
1840	Virtuoso Niccolo Paganini dies in Nice, France. Paganini is arguably the greatest violin player of all time. Besides having perfect intonation and absolute pitch, he introduces numerous innovative techniques and ways of playing his instrument.
1845	Leopold Auer is born in Veszprém, Hungary. A talented violinist, conductor, and composer, he is best known for his teaching methods. His famous pupils include Efrem Zimbalist, Mischa Elman, and Jascha Heifetz.
1875	Fritz Kreisler, who would become one of the most famous violin players of his day, is born in Vienna, Austria.
1908	David Fiodorovich Oistrakh is born in the Ukraine. Throughout his life, Oistrakh would make numerous recordings of violin works. His recording of Beethoven's Triple Concerto is particularly well known.
1923	Child prodigy Yehudi Menuhin gains widespread popularity with his public performance of Eduardo Lalo's "Spanish Symphony."
1959	Rudolf Koelman is born in Amsterdam. He first studies violin under Jan Bor, and by age 13 is enrolled into the Conservatory of Amsterdam. Aside from being a very productive recording artist, TV and radio performer, he performs worldwide as a soloist and chamber musician.
1980	The documentary *From Mao to Mozart*, chronicling a historic year-long teaching tour of China by the great violin player Isaac Stern, wins an Academy Award.
1987	Jascha Heifetz, widely considered the greatest violinist of the 20th century, dies in Los Angeles.
2006	In celebration of the 250th anniversary of Wolfgang Amadeus Mozart's birth, award-winning violinist Augustin Dumay plays a series of concerts on three continents.

INTERNET RESOURCES

http://www.menc.org

The mission of the National Association for Music Education is to "advance music education by encouraging the study and making of music by all." Go to this site for more information and articles related to issues in music education, making a donation, and how you can become a member.

http://musiced.about.com/od/beginnersguide/bb/bviolin.htm

At this website you'll find a list of helpful tips for buying your first violin.

http://www.8notes.com

A great resource for all musicians, this site has violin sheet music for 76 songs available for free download, along with fingering charts, a glossary of music terms, a free online metronome, and links to other useful music websites.

http://www.ibreathemusic.com

An invaluable resource for any musician, this site has forums and articles covering a wide range of music-related topics, including composition, improvisation, and ear training.

http://www.centrum.is/hansi/maintenance

Here you'll see a highly informative article describing, in detail, how to care for your violin.

http://www.violinonline.com
    This website has online lessons and free sheet music for violin enthu-
    siasts of all ages and levels of experience.

http://www.classical.net
    Classical Net has reviews of over 4000 CDs and DVDs (among other
    media), as well as files and links to thousands of other related web-
    sites.

http://www.theviolinsite.com
    The Violin Site website offers video instruction for beginning and
    advanced violinists as well as help with violin technique and violin
    practice exercises.

http://www.violinist.com/
    An online community of violinists. This site includes frequently asked
    questions, discussion boards, and blogs of interest to violin players.

GLOSSARY

Accidental—a sharp, flat, or natural note that occurs in a piece of music but is not indicated in the key signature.

Bar lines—these vertical lines mark the division between measures of music.

Beat—the pulse of the music, which is usually implied using the combination of accented and unaccented notes throughout the composition.

Chord—three or more different tones played at the same time.

Clef (bass and treble)—located on the left side of each line of music, these symbols indicate the names and pitch of the notes corresponding to their lines and spaces.

Eighth note—a note with a solid oval, a stem, and a single tail that has 1/8 the value of a whole note.

Enharmonic notes—notes that are written differently in a musical score, but have the same pitch when played (for example, F# and Gb).

Flat sign (b)—a symbol that indicates that the note following it should be lowered by one half step. This remains in effect for an entire measure, unless otherwise indicated by a natural sign.

Half note—a note with a hollow oval and stem that has 1/2 the value of a whole note.

Half step—a unit of measurement in music that is the smallest distance between two notes, either ascending or descending. An octave is divided equally into 12 half steps.

Interval—the distance in pitch between two tones, indicated using half and whole steps.

Key signature—found between the clef and time signature, it describes which notes to play with sharps or flats throughout a piece of music.

Measure—a unit of music contained between two adjacent bar lines.

Music staff—the horizontal lines and spaces between and upon which music is written.

Natural sign—a symbol which instructs that a note should not be played as a sharp or a flat.

Notes—written or printed symbols which represent the frequency and duration of tones contained in a piece of music.

Octave—a relationship between two pitches where one tone has double (or half) the frequency of the other.

Pitch—the perceived highness or lowness of a sound or tone.

Quarter note—a note with a solid oval and a stem that is played for 1/4 of the duration of a whole note.

Repeat sign—a pair of vertical dots that appear near bar lines that indicate a section of music that is to be played more than once.

Rest—a figure that is used to denote silence for a given duration in a piece of music.

Scale—a sequence of notes in order of pitch in ascending or descending order.

Sharp sign (#)—this symbol indicates that the note following it should be raised by one half-step. This remains in effect for an entire measure, unless otherwise indicated by a natural sign.

Tempo—the speed at which music is to be played. It is notated by either a word describing the relative speed of the piece or by the number of beats per minute (B.P.M.) that occur as it is played.

Time signature—located to the right of the clef and key signatures, the top digit indicates the number of beats per measure, and the number at the bottom shows which kind of note receives one beat.

Tone—a distinct musical sound which can be produced by a voice or instrument.

Whole note—a note indicated by a hollow oval without a stem. It has the longest time value and represents a length of 4 beats when written in 4/4 time.

Whole step—a unit of measurement in music that is equal to two half steps.

INDEX

ABOUT THE AUTHOR

Frank Cappelli is a warm, engaging artist, who possesses the special ability to transform the simple things of life into a wonderful musical experience. He has had an impressive career since receiving a B.A. in music education from West Chester State College (now West Chester University). Frank has performed his music at many American venues—from Disney World in Florida to Knott's Berry Farm in California—as well as in Ireland, Spain, France, and Italy. He has also performed with the Detroit Symphony, the Buffalo Philharmonic, the Pittsburgh Symphony, and the Chattanooga Symphony.

In 1987, Frank created Peanut Heaven, a record label for children. The following year, he worked with WTAE-TV in Pittsburgh to develop *Cappelli and Company*, an award winning children's television variety show. The weekly program premiered in 1989, and is now internationally syndicated.

In 1989, Frank signed a contract with A&M Records, which released his four albums for children (*Look Both Ways, You Wanna Be a Duck?, On Vacation,* and *Good*) later that year. *Pass the Coconut* was released by A&M in 1991. *Take a Seat* was released in September of 1993. With the 1990 A&M Video release of *All Aboard the Train and Other Favorites* and *Slap Me Five*, Cappelli's popular television program first became available to kids nationwide. Both videos have received high marks from a number of national publications, including *People Magazine, Video Insider, Billboard, USA Today, Entertainment Weekly,* and *TV Guide.*

Frank has received many awards, including the Parent's Choice Gold Award, regional Emmy Awards, the Gabriel Award for Outstanding Achievement in Children's Programming, and the Achievement in Children's Television Award. He is a three-time recipient of the Pennsylvania Association of Broadcasters' award for Best Children's Program in Pennsylvania.

787.2
CAP